SECRET
LOUISIANA

Chris Champagne

JONGLEZ PUBLISHING

Travel guides

We have taken great pleasure in drawing up *Secret Louisiana – An unusual guide* and hope that through its guidance you will, like us, continue to discover unusual, hidden or little-known aspects of the region.

Descriptions of certain places are accompanied by thematic sections highlighting historical details or anecdotes as an aid to understanding the region in all its complexity.

Secret Louisiana – An unusual guide also draws attention to the multitude of details found in places that we may pass every day without noticing. This is an invitation to look more closely at the urban landscape and, more generally, it is a means of seeing our own region with the curiosity and attention that we often display while travelling elsewhere ...

Comments on this guide and its contents, as well as information on sites not mentioned, are welcome and will help us to enrich future editions.

Don't hesitate to contact us:
Email: info@jonglezpublishing.com

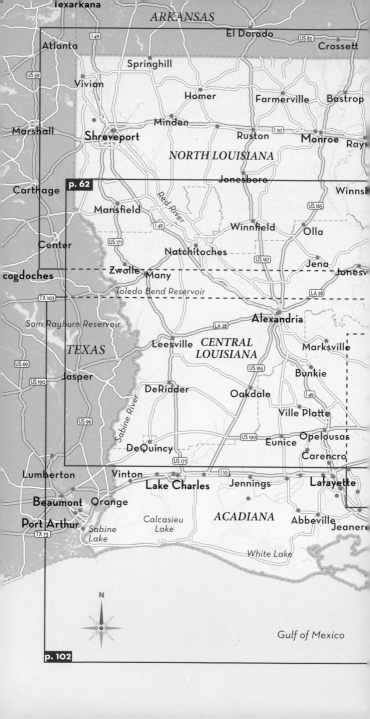

CONTENTS

North Louisiana

Central Louisiana

Acadiana

CONTENTS

Florida Parishes

CONTENTS

Greater New Orleans

- 13 -

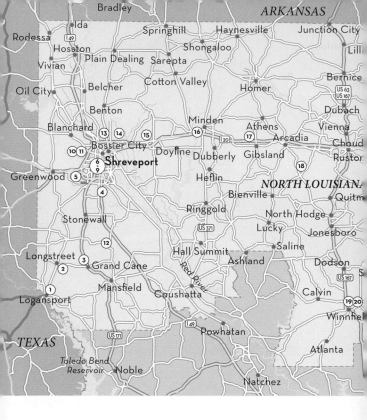

North Louisiana

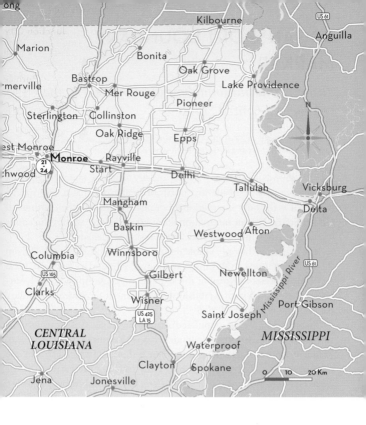

LOGANSPORT BOUNDARY MARKER

The only international boundary marker in the continental United States

8149 Highway FM 31 near to Texas–Louisiana border
Near the intersection of Louisiana Highway 765, Logansport

The boundary marker that sits quietly inside a metal fence on a remote rural roadside just north of Logansport has a very special feature: It is the only international boundary marker in the continental United States. Yes, an international boundary marker within the country, not one showing the border with Mexico or Canada!

The marker is the only visible remnant of a project that reached from the Gulf of Mexico to Arkansas, marking the boundary between Texas and United States territory in the 19th century. On April 3, 1841, surveyors were tasked with establishing a permanent recognized boundary between the U.S. and Mexico.

But in 1836, Texas, populated mainly by Anglo-American settlers, seceded from Mexico. Its independence was recognized in 1837 by U.S. President Andrew Jackson, and by France in 1839 (which explains the existence, still today, of a plaque in Paris recalling the location of the Texas embassy in France – see *Secret Paris*, also published by Jonglez).

The independent Republic of Texas (which roughly corresponded to

the eastern half of present-day Texas) lasted nine years, until December 29, 1845, when Texas was finally incorporated into the United States, becoming the 28th American state. This annexation led to the Mexican-American War (1846–48).

The surveying of the border from the Gulf of Mexico up the middle of the Sabine River extended up to the Red River, where Louisiana meets Arkansas.

The first marker at the Gulf of Mexico was a 36-ft. pole erected in an earthen mound. Due to erosion and exposure to the elements such as hurricanes and floods, the only remaining marker along the Sabine today is the one north of Logansport on Louisiana Highway 765.

In 1976, during the bicentennial celebrations of American independence, a bronze marker to explain the significance of the boundary marker was erected by the Desoto Parish Historical Society.

The surveying of the Sabine Boundary had great historical significance and resulted from the 1819 Adams-Onís Treaty, also known as the Transcontinental Treaty or the Purchase of Florida Accord as it also gave possession of Florida to the United States. U.S. Secretary of State John Quincy Adams and the Spanish ambassador to the U.S., Luis de Onís, negotiated the treaty. Both countries wanted to avoid the territorial conflicts that they feared could erupt from the instability of governance in the area.

The line between the United States and Texas was vaguely defined by prior agreements. Subsequently, it led outlaws and other miscreants to use what was initially designated as neutral ground but became notoriously known as "No Man's Land" because it was an area without law. Fugitives from both governments would escape to this area and terrorize citizens almost at will; the boundary was designed, among other things, to put an end to this lawlessness.

In 1841, many years after the Adams-Onís Treaty had established the boundary as the Sabine River, engineers and surveyors set about operations to mark the border. But the remote, swampy conditions were extremely harsh and it took over a year to complete the mission.

GRAVE OF MOSES ROSE

The only survivor of the Alamo

Ferguson Cemetery Highway 168 on Funston Road, Funston

Near Logansport in Desoto Parish, in a remote family cemetery in Funston, lies the grave of Moses Rose, the only survivor of the Alamo. According to some accounts, Moses Rose – born Louis Rose in France – was given the nickname Moses at the Alamo because he was one of the oldest fighters at the age of 51. His story has a legendary but problematic provenance.

As the story goes, Rose participated in the Fredonian Rebellion (the first attempt by Texans to secede from Mexico) and the siege of Béxar (when a volunteer Texan army defeated Mexican forces). He was then one of Jim Bowie's contingent at the Alamo, fighting there for ten days.

As the Mexican army surrounded the men at the Alamo fighting for Texas' independence from Mexico, Santa Ana, the Mexican general, raised a flag of "No quarters," which indicated that he intended to kill all the men at the Alamo if his forces were victorious.

At this point in the story – as told by Moses Rose in subsequent years – Colonel Travis, the leader of the Americans at the Alamo, drew a line in the sand with his sword: Anyone who wanted to leave should cross the line before the decisive battle. Rose initially refused to cross the line even though he was encouraged to do so by Travis, probably in deference to his age. Rose is said to have been the only man who crossed the line later that night, becoming the only person at the Alamo to survive because he left before the battle.

In later years, Rose would not shy away from the fact that he left and would talk freely about his role in the Alamo saga. Asked why he left, his answer is said to have been, "I wasn't ready to die."

His story has many doubters, but in 1939, a Texas archivist named Robert Balk found documents that lent credence to Rose's tale. After escaping from the Alamo, Rose ended up at the farm of one William P. Zuber, the source of much of the Moses Rose tale.

In the years after the famous battle, Rose served as a witness for many families, verifying who perished at the Alamo for official documents related to land disputes and other property claims.

Rose was not a stranger to military life as some accounts claim that he was a lieutenant in Napoleon's army and had fought with the French in Italy, Portugal, and Russia.

A 1953 film, *The Man from the Alamo*, starred Glenn Ford as a Rose-like figure.

MANSFIELD FEMALE COLLEGE MUSEUM

A poignant look into our past

101 Monroe Street, Mansfield
318-871-9978
visitnomansland.com/listing/mansfield-female-college-museum
Tue–Thurs 9am–4pm

A gem that offers a poignant look into our past, the well-maintained Mansfield Female College Museum gives a glimpse into the once-thriving women's college and some lagniappe, as the building once served as a hospital for war-wounded during the Civil War.

The Mansfield Female College was a pioneer as the first college for women founded west of the Mississippi. It carried on for 50 years, educating young ladies in art, science and foreign languages.

Several artifacts and documents have been donated to the museum, mainly by townsfolk and former students. Yearbooks, class rings, photos and documents pertaining to the school, such as tuition ledgers, offer an interesting peek into the past.

There is a replica of what would have been a typical girls' dorm circa 1920. The room is a bit sparse yet contains the essentials of college life: exquisitely preserved party dresses, a bed, a vanity table, a baby cradle with a doll, a college pennant on the wall, and a typewriter on the small desk.

The highlight for many may be the role played by the college in the Battle of Mansfield, an important Civil War battle that raged within hearing distance of the college just outside of Mansfield. The wounded were brought here, and the building served as a military hospital.

A room filled with artifacts of the wounded and those who treated them has a sobering effect. There is a patient's bed, a glass case with medical tools of the time (including a surgeon's amputation kit consisting of a few items, most notably two saws), hypodermic needles for the limited drugs available, a wooden box displaying bullets with teeth marks on them as they were used to help the wounded endure the pain at a time when painkillers were often in short supply ... giving an all-too-real meaning to the phrase "bite the bullet."

There is also a case with an authentic peg leg and a gruesome-looking metal hook used to help soldiers retrieve the dead bodies of their comrades from the battlefield.

Blood that stained the floors

The central room where you enter the museum has an antique rug, but the wooden floor under it is said to be darker than all the other floors due to the amount of blood that stained the floors over 150 years ago when the place was a military hospital.

There is a small tribute to a native son, Joshua Logan, tucked away in a hall. Logan was an important figure in American show business in the 20th century as the director of many prominent Broadway plays and Hollywood films. He directed South Pacific on Broadway and also the Hollywood film version.

HUGE MAILBOX

An oil rags-to-riches story

Mile 187 on Interstate 49, Frierson
Newellton mailbox, 3 miles north of Newellton

At mile marker 187 (on your right as you travel north toward Shreveport, near Frierson), a 19-ft. mailbox looks toward Interstate 49. You might think it's impossible to miss such a giant object, but if you don't know it's there (and it's highly visible), it can blend in as you tool along at plus 70 mph. If you get off at the exit, you can drive to the mailbox and get a closer look as it sits high up on a ridge.

The mailbox was a "statement" by the Dowden family, who were featured in the TV show "Bayou Billionaires." It's a recognition of the enormous checks the family received for natural gas found on their property.

The family already had four natural gas wells working on their land, bringing them in a few thousand dollars a month, but the new wells are thought to have netted them $40,000 a month at the time the TV show debuted on Country Music Television. According to press reports, the price of natural gas in 2012 (when the big mailbox was constructed) was depressed, but if the price ever rose again to 2008 levels, those $40,000 checks would balloon to a million dollars a month.

The show was billed as a typical "working-class family striking it rich" story. The family, as well as the producers, insist that they did not strive to make a redneck show and, indeed, some of the sad realities of life that affect us all were avoided in the plotlines. The Dowdens and the show's producers did not strive to exploit every opportunity to shock or titillate, as many reality shows do.

The plotlines did not delve into topics that could be seen as more voyeuristic, like the fact that the Dowdens' daughter was diagnosed with multiple sclerosis. (She insisted that this should not be revealed in the show.) Sadly, she was later murdered – allegedly by a jealous romantic partner – which adds a tragic twist to this rags-to-riches story.

The Dowdens' natural gas wealth was made possible by new fracking techniques, and this has caused consternation among environmentalists: Fracking is a process in which vast amounts of water are flushed into the ground horizontally to free up any natural gas trapped in the shale. Environmentalists contend that natural gas can contaminate drinking water and that the fracking process can cause earthquakes.

Still, the story of vast amounts of money springing from natural resources overnight is a compelling narrative that gives daydreamers hope. On the side of an Interstate highway, the kitschy mailbox symbol is a tangible sign of that hope.

There is another massive mailbox in Louisiana near Newellton, but this one is only 14 ft. high. It also provides a nice photo op – you can take advantage of it when you pass along US Highway 65.

CHIMP HAVEN

The world's largest chimpanzee sanctuary

13600 Chimpanzee Place, Keithville
318-925-9575
chimphaven.org
By appointment only

Deep in the woods of northwestern Louisiana, about 22 miles southwest of Shreveport, the very special Chimp Haven is the world's largest chimpanzee sanctuary.

Although the facility is not usually open to the public, each year there are a few small windows for the general public to visit during Chimpanzee Discovery days. As the day is officially only from 9am to noon, it's imperative to plan ahead if you wish to visit this wonderful place.

There are other unique opportunities to see the chimps up close. For example, a special tour called Chimp Chat is offered to groups of ten or more: It allows you to see the chimpanzees going about their daily business, with presentations by the staff to explain the lives of the threatened primates and the facility's mission.

There is also a photographic opportunity for both professional and amateur photographers, but again, reservations are required as only six photographers are allowed on any given day.

Chimp Haven welcomed its first two residents in 2005. At any given time, there are between 300 and 400 chimpanzees living out their lives in a way that allows them to choose how their day will be spent (climbing trees, gathering and eating their favorite fruit, roaming through the forested area, and bonding in large groups as chimpanzees are very social animals).

The average age of the chimpanzees at Chimp Haven is 34, with some living well into their 60s.

In the 1980s scientists, animal behavioralists, and the U.S. government realized that the medical research being carried out on chimpanzees to help eradicate AIDS and hepatitis (and other diseases) was leading to a situation where there would be an aging population of chimps.

A coalition of the government, animal behavioralists, zoos, veterinarians, animal rights advocates, pharmaceutical firms, and others met to address this problem. In 1995, they founded Chimp Haven, Inc. In 2000 the U.S. Congress passed the Chimpanzee Health Improvement, Maintenance, and Protection Act (CHIMP) to create a sanctuary for research animals and privately owned chimpanzees as well as chimpanzees from the entertainment world. The Caddo Parish Commission of Northwest Louisiana donated 200 wooded acres of the Eddie D. Jones Nature Park.

Chimp Haven's mission is "to provide and promote the best care of sanctuary chimpanzees and inspire action for the species worldwide."

The U.S. government pays 75% of the cost of running Chimp Haven; the other 25% comes from the private sector and individual contributors.

SHREVEPORT WATER WORKS MUSEUM

A true five-star hidden gem for fans of industrial equipment and engineering

142 North Common Street, Shreveport
318-221-3388
shreveportwaterworks.org/waterworks-museum/
gerald.forrest@sos.la.gov
Tue–Sat 10am–4pm
Free admission

Once known as the McNeill Street Pumping Station, the Shreveport Water Works Museum is a unique spot – a true five-star hidden gem with an intact steam-powered system that once provided clean drinking water to Shreveport. It is an incredible find for those interested in industrial equipment and engineering.

Opened in 1887, the plant added a filtering system in 1890 when this was cutting-edge technology, and in 1911 it became one of the first facilities in the country to add liquid chlorine to the pumping system. The facility and pumps here were so efficient that they were not taken offline until 1980 – until that time, it had been the only remaining operational steam-powered plant in the country.

Large iron wheels, massive steam-powered equipment, settling basins, and all the bells and whistles of such a plant are still in working order.

Today the building is a National Historic Landmark and National Historic Civil Engineering Landmark. It is also a prime example of Victorian-era industrial architecture, with 6-ft.-deep brick walls and bolted roof rafters, iron-cast windows, brick archways, and wood and metal pitched roofs. It was built to last.

Today in addition to an audio tour available by app, a friendly docent is here to answer questions. Or you can meander on your own to marvel at this over 130-year-old piece of 19th-century engineering ingenuity. As you return to the Victorian era, you will appreciate the engineers and scientists who paved the way for things we take for granted in modern society, such as clean drinking water.

The impetus of the system can be traced back to a series of fires in Shreveport and the need to have the pumping capacity to fight such disasters, as well as the city's desire to have indoor plumbing.

The plant was initially built and updated by private enterprise franchisees. It was turned over to Shreveport in 1917 in line with the trend of municipalities taking over public utilities.

Blow the whistle

One cool feature of the museum is the steam-powered whistle that once was used to warn the city of fires. With permission, you can still blow the whistle to hear the shrill warning burst.

AMERICAN MUSEUM OF FENCING

An absolute jewel of a find

1413 Fairfield Avenue, Shreveport
318-227-7575
museumofamericanfencing.com
Mon–Thurs 3pm–8pm, Sat 9am–noon

In a Tudor-style building just off of Interstate 20, near Shreveport's downtown area, the American Museum of Fencing is an absolute jewel of a find. As you walk in, you find a riot for the eyes: trophies, colorful international fencing uniforms, medals, cases with all sorts of interesting and unusual memorabilia. The racks of fencing masks might even lead you to believe that this is the clubhouse of the Three Musketeers.

Most people would probably ask, "How did the American Fencing Museum end up in Shreveport, Louisiana?" The answer is one of the most curious aspects of the place, which is also a vibrant, active fencing school run by Andy Shaw.

Andy is the official historian of the American Fencing Association and owns the most extensive private collection of fencing memorabilia in the United States. Coupled with the fact that he has a vast knowl-

edge of fencing facts and lore, he is the perfect person to be entrusted with running the museum. Andy is a friendly, knowledgeable, extremely likable and accomplished soul, and if you get there before the students arrive, he will be happy to take the time to chat a bit about the museum.

The memorabilia is mesmerizing to those who know the art and sport, and can be equally of interest to those who know little about fencing but have a keen interest in history.

Born in Manhattan, Andy lived next to the fencing star Edward Vebell. At the age of eight, with Vebell's sponsorship, Andy got his first lessons in the sport from Csaba Elthes, who was a six-time coach of the American Olympic fencing team. Andy then found himself coached by Giorgio Santelli, the Olympic Gold Medal winner for Italy in 1920, and himself a five-time coach of the American fencing team.

Andy eventually became an all-American fencer at Temple University and then a top fencing official in the United States, officiating at many national events. He moved to Los Angeles, where his expertise and talents were sought out as a stage combat expert for the film industry. Andy has coached Bob Dylan, Russell Crowe, Kiefer Sutherland, Blair Underwood, Mia Sara, Jimmy Buffet and Beau Bridges, among many others, in theatrical swordsmanship.

Today Andy has found his way to Shreveport, where he trains young fencers and runs this most interesting of places.

WIENER BROTHERS
INTERNATIONAL STYLE HOUSES

Louisiana's first International Style residences

Ed Wile House, 626 Wilder Place, Shreveport
Jacques Wiener House, 622 Longleaf Road
David Flesh House, 415 Sherwood Road

The Ed Wile House, in the Southern Highland neighborhood of Shreveport, displays the crisp lines, rectilinear forms and taut, flat plain surfaces devoid of ornamentation that are the trademarks of the residential International Style. It was also known for using materials readily available at the end of the 19th century, such as cheap iron and steel and prefabricated concrete, all of which changed the face of modern architecture.

Here in Shreveport, Samuel and William Weiner, two of the earliest proponents of the style in the United States, blazed a trail by designing and building Louisiana's first International Style residences.

Inspired by a visit to Europe, and by the works of German Walter Gropius with his Bauhaus style, Ludwig Mies van der Rohe in the Netherlands and Le Corbusier in France (Samuel Weiner and his wife Mabel traveled to Europe in the early 1930s), the Wieners soon established themselves in northwestern Louisiana. Their modern, spare, geometric buildings became known in Shreveport and its environs as Wiener Houses.

Today the Ed Wile House, the Jacques Wiener House, and the David Flesh House are the three masterpieces of the Weiner brothers' residential work. Still part of the Shreveport residential landscape, they have been restored to their original state and are beautifully maintained.

In 1939, *Architectural Forum* magazine dedicated an issue to 50 homes in the United States that had been built for around $5,000. The John S. Preston House, another Weiner Brothers home at 22 Jordan Street, was one of them.

The International Style that became the dominant style of Western architecture was driven by the desire to have buildings that served a functional purpose; it led to the construction of skyscrapers that still dot the skylines of modern cities. This was a response to the rapid industrialization of contemporary society and was facilitated by new technologies and materials such as glass and reinforced concrete.

Some other residential works of note by the Weiner brothers are the Samuel G. Weiner House at 615 Longleaf Road and The William Weiner House at 2 Longleaf Lane. The brothers designed civic buildings, including the Shreveport Municipal Auditorium at 705 Grand Avenue, and schools of note, including J. S. Clark Junior High at 351 Hearn Avenue and Woodlawn High School at 7340 Wyngate Boulevard.

PIONEER HERITAGE CENTER

A unique glimpse into daily plantation life

1 University Place, Shreveport
318-797-5339
lsus.edu/community/pioneer-heritage-center
pioneer@lsus.edu
Tours by appointment only

Sitting alone at the rear of the LSU-Shreveport campus, the Pioneer Heritage Center can easily be overlooked. However, the seven plantation structures brought from various parts of Louisiana, with Caspiana House (known as the Big House) as the centerpiece, serve as a unique, well-kept attraction with an educational mission.

Most of the plantations that once lined the Mississippi, as well as other landlocked plantations, did not have cinematic mansions like Tara from *Gone with The Wind*, but were well-built smaller mansions such as the one found here. In fact, they are more representative of daily plantation life.

Sitting on a high pier as it once did on the banks of the Mississippi in case of flooding, Caspiana House is the focal point of the intimate complex. The entrance foyer is flanked by a well-appointed parlor of the period and a typical plantation bedroom with a four-poster bed and other accoutrements from a wealthy landowner's daily life.

Among the unique period pieces is a rare item in the parlor: a lamp/Victrola. Still in working order, visitors can hear records from the 1920s that give a feel of home entertainment at the time.

The grounds boast the Thrasher House, a refurbished dogtrot house: It is about as fine a specimen of a dogtrot house as can be found anywhere. The Blacksmith Shop has working tools and equipment in an authentic log structure built in the 1880s. The office of Dr. Hartwell Lockwood Alison – brought from Caspiana, where it was still in use as late as the 1930s – serves to illustrate the medical practices of the time. There is also a detached kitchen, which was functional well into the 1930s: It is typical of plantation life as the building stood on its own to prevent fires from consuming the main house. Additionally, the Webb & Webb Commissary has a rich inventory of goods, offering a glimpse of a typical plantation store of a century ago.

Another staple of plantation life, the Riverfront Mission of First Baptist Church, was moved to the Pioneer Heritage Center from the Batture in Shreveport, where it once served a community of hobos, the homeless, and other transients along the unclaimed banks of the river.

The Pioneer Heritage Center has received a commendation for excellence from the American Association for State and Local History for its progressive educational presentations. Schoolchildren troop through on tours throughout the year.

FORT HUMBUG LOG CANNON

A charred log disguised to look like a cannon

400 East Stoner Avenue, Shreveport

At an intersection in Shreveport, in a grassy setting, a lone black log cannon sits almost unseen by commuters. It remains a piece of Civil War lore and a tribute to human ingenuity or, at the very least, a good try. If you look carefully, you'll see that it's not a cannon at all but a charred log disguised to look like a lethal artillery piece. Amazingly, these type of cannons were used at Fort Humbug (the nickname that stuck for Fort Turnbull), one of the fortifications the Confederate Army threw up to protect Shreveport from Union attack after the town became capital of the Confederacy in 1863.

The Red River was a vital theater of the Civil War in the West because of supply lines that went all the way to Mexico, where the Confederates had successfully sidestepped the very successful central blockades that the Union had enjoyed throughout the war.

Major General Nathaniel Banks was in command of the Union forces in Louisiana. His reputation as a political appointee, not a military man, lends credence (if not substance) to the tale that these charred logs (including the one still in Shreveport) helped the Confederate cause. It sits at a traffic intersection near a U.S. Veterans Hospital.

Shreveport was vital but not well fortified. However, General Banks' intelligence and reconnaissance led him to think otherwise.

The Confederate forces at Fort Turnbull knew that the Union forces and navy would outgun them, so they devised a dubious plan that could easily be mistaken for a B comedy film script: They cut down trees and fashioned the logs to look like cannons. The Confederates painted the logs black or charred them to make them look like iron cannons. They then set them up on ramparts to fool the Union into thinking they were ready to repel an assault.

Confederate General John B. Magruder said of the plan, "That's not going to work; that's a humbug." It did work, however. The Union forces turned back, or so the story goes, and the name Fort Humbug has stuck.

ZOMBIE HALL OF FAME SIGN

The work of a lively sense of humor

Near the corner of Spring Street and Crockett Street, Shreveport

Near the corner of Spring Street and Crockett Street in Shreveport, a blue sign with white lettering crowned by an outline of the skyline of Shreveport looks like your average run-of-the-mill directional graphic to help visitors find local landmarks.

But this sign on the 200 block of Crockett Street shows the way to the Government Plaza, the Parish Courthouse ... and the Zombie

Hall of Fame. Yes, the Zombie Hall of Fame! Not to worry about investigating the destination; It's just the work of a lively sense of humor. There is no Zombie Hall of Fame. Drat!

The culprit responsible is unknown, but some say it was a local bartender. Others say that when the authorities discovered the bogus directions to the nonexistent Zombie Hall of Fame, the ingenuity of the thing and the skill of mimicking the other authentic signs led the powers-that-be to leave the sign alone.

Another "authentic" sign

In 2015, a yellow and black street sign that again mimicked the real traffic signage color scheme was erected on Texas Avenue, saying "Godzilla Crossing." The crossing sign had it spelled out and a very nice black outline of Godzilla on a yellow background.

When the Louisiana Department of Transportation and Development became aware of the sign, they removed it from the utility pole it was attached to. A spokesperson for the department issued this explanation: "If a situation arose where someone was driving through and looked at the sign and was distracted by it and crashed, we could be held liable."

ROCK CHAPEL

A contemplative chapel nestled in the woods

1746 Smithport Lake Road, Mansfield
318-872-1158
stjoseph@nwcable.net
As you drive down the small country highway, you'll come to an archway that says 'Rock Chapel.' Drive through the archway to reach the chapel at the end of a quarter-mile gravel road

Off the beaten path for sure, on a hill beautifully framed by nature, a peaceful spiritual rock chapel is clearly worth a detour for its simplicity and beauty.

Louisiana was first populated by Europeans in the late 17th century and Natchitoches, which is close to the chapel, was the oldest European settlement in the state. The Spanish and French first brought Catholicism to this part of the world and established churches in the area. Yet German Catholics from Texas in 1886 created the Carmelite monastery that once stood here in this peaceful and remote forest.

The monks and priests of the religious community wished to have a contemplative chapel to practice their faith: Monks from the Carmelite monastery took rocks from the area and, using mud for the masonry, built this simple yet exquisite timeless chapel that people can still enjoy today.

Over the years, the chapel has been used for weddings and Easter services. The interior is adorned with frescoes and murals painted by a French priest while he lived at the monastery. They were restored in the 1960s, but as the chapel is now padlocked, the beautiful murals are unfortunately unavailable for viewing by the general public. You may contact St. Joseph's Catholic Church or the Desoto Tourist Office to see if and when viewing might be resumed.

The monastery and church connected to the chapel burned down in 1904 and today the chapel is maintained and operated by St. Joseph's.

> Take a concrete walkway up the hill, cross a creek over a small bridge, and you'll see some of the former monks' graves flanking the sidewalk.

WILLIS-KNIGHTON TALBOT MEDICAL MUSEUM

A little-known showcase of vintage medical equipment

2105 Airline Drive, Bossier City
318-212-8472 – museum.wkhs.com
Free admission
By appointment only

Visible only by appointment, the Willis-Knighton Talbot Medical Museum is one of the least-known museums in the state. Embedded in the Willis-Knighton Innovation Center, a facility at the forefront of medical education, the museum showcases vintage medical equipment. The intimate exhibits allow visitors to get an up-close look at the lifesaving innovations of early and mid-20th-century medicine.

The docent-led tour starts with a look at a lovingly restored Reconstruction-era doctors' buggy, followed by an overview of the development of modern medicine, with an emphasis on the Shreveport area.

The highlights of the museum – of great interest to almost anyone in the medical field but also to those who have a keen sense of history – are the once "modern" versions of an operating room, obstetric

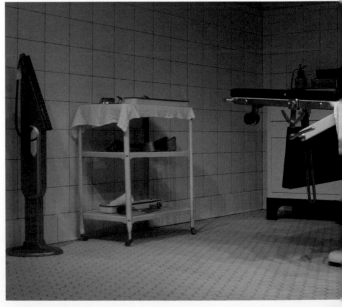

equipment, an anesthesia machine, and even a tool kit of stainless-steel medical instruments from World War II.

The museum has a large exhibit dedicated to the Yellow Fever epidemic of 1873, an eerie echo of the Covid pandemic. Half the population in Shreveport contracted Yellow Fever during the epidemic and half of them died.

One of the most fascinating exhibits honors the career of Dr. Siporah S. Turner, an African American woman who graduated with honors from Meharry Medical School in Nashville in 1907 and practiced in Shreveport, specializing in women's health. She also ran a nursing school with her mother, Delilah Robinson.

Another exhibit honors the nurses of Shreveport. Yet another is a display of patent medicines: It is eye-opening as these elixirs were popular in U.S. society as late as the 1950s, claiming to cure all ailments when in reality they had no effect whatsoever.

The museum is located in a brand-new facility providing state-of-the-art instruction for medical and nursing students. Virtual patients simulate seizures, bleeding, and a full range of real-world reactions that give medical students a true feel for the emotional aspect of practicing and providing medical treatment for real people.

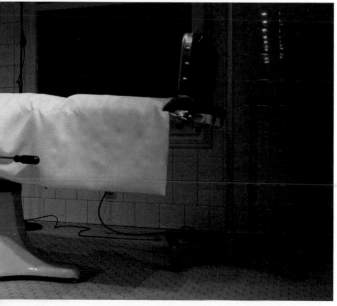

BARKSDALE GLOBAL POWER MUSEUM

The highest and fastest jet aircraft ever

88 Shreveport Road, Barksdale AFB, Bossier City
318-456-2840
Mon–Fri 9am–3pm
barksdaleglobalpowermuseum.com
The home of the 2nd Bomb Wing and the 8th Air Force, Barksdale is a working military installation and visits must be planned at least 30 days in advance
Go online to fill out the forms (There is a special form for non-U.S. citizens)

The huge area of one of the most important military airfields in the world obscures the fact that it is home to a museum open to the public. The air park is in plain sight, yet it blends into the surroundings as the working base hums around it.

On Barksdale Air Force Base (which can be visited despite being an active military base), the Barksdale Global Power Museum consists of a spectacular air park with an impressive collection of bombers and other planes. The museum ensemble is completed by a smaller building, adjacent to the air park, that holds several exhibits chronicling the history of the U.S. Air Force.

Among the exhibits are an art gallery of paintings of the various warplanes, uniforms from across the years worn by aviators, missiles, photographs of the planes and flyers, and a World War II briefing room with a video of Barksdale's history along with artifacts associated with the history of aerial warfare.

One of the most popular and unique exhibits is the actual podium at which President George W. Bush addressed the nation and the world with his speech on September 11, 2001, about the momentous events of that fateful day. Visitors can stand at the podium at the exact same spot, and in front of the very same flag and clock.

The museum is dedicated to the U.S. Air Force and to the defense of the nation and its allies, but it also aims to stress the peacetime history of Barksdale. According to the website, the museum is "not only a memorial to our successes in battle, but a recognition of the many years spent training to deter war. The peacetime history of Barksdale Air Force Base is as significant as those years at war."

The air park – whose collection includes a *B-17, B-24, B-52D, B-52G Stratofortress, P-51 Mustang, B-1B bomber* and the *MACH 3+ SR-71 Blackbird*, the highest and fastest flying jet aircraft ever – gives an idea of the visual impact of these fighting machines. A *Titan 11* nose cone and an *AGM-28 Hound Dog* missile are also on display.

The museum was opened in 1979 thanks to the efforts of Buck Rigg, and the B-17 was the first plane in what is now the air park. It was initially called the 8th Air Force Museum, but as there was another museum with a similar name in Georgia, it was renamed the Barksdale Global Power Museum in 2012.

Barksdale is home to the 2nd Bomb Wing (the oldest bomb wing in the USAF) and to the Air Force Global Strike Command. It is also home to dozens of state-of-the-art bombers such as the B52-H Stratofortress and is a key training base for all Stratofortress crews.

TOUCHSTONE WILDLIFE & ART MUSEUM

An incredible taxidermy museum … and a bit more

3386 Louisiana Highway 80, Haughton
318-949-2323
touchstonemuseum.com
June–August: Tue–Sat 10am–4:30pm
September–May: Thurs–Sat 10am–4:30pm
Admission charge

As you're driving down Louisiana Highway 70 near Haughton, just in case you miss the 7-ft. brown bear, or the two life-size giraffes, or the zebras with their heads some 11 ft. above the ground propped up on poles, there is a sign on the building in 8-ft.-high letters that reads "MUSEUM".

Although you might not associate giraffes with rural northern Louisiana, nonetheless, here they are. This is the Touchstone Wildlife & Art Museum. There's a lot of wildlife to be found inside, and of course, as most of us have heard, art is in the eye of the beholder.

Sam Touchstone, a taxidermist, created this incredible place over 40 years ago, and although he's no longer with us, his showpiece of artistry (perhaps obsession?), craftsmanship, and just whimsy carries on.

First, of course, are the animals. Skillful state-of-the-art taxidermy leads many people to refer to the place as the taxidermy museum. It is that and a bit more. The animals were mainly acquired from zoos after they had died and were then put into the hands of Sam and other taxidermists, with spectacular results. Most of the animals are shown in very natural poses, and the expressions on their faces are so well done that you can't help being impressed.

You'll find a family of foxes playing while mom looks on, a honey badger from Africa, lions, panthers, giraffes, bisons and birds of all sorts, often backed up by beautiful artwork done by local professional artists to give a great feeling of authenticity.

There is, however, much more than just animals. There are small exhibits about the Civil War, World War II, and the Old West, a shrunken head, rocks that glow in the dark, a wild honey-bee hive, an elephant skull, and even a cut-out of John Wayne that invites you to take a photo with the Duke.

And, oh yeah, a photo of James Tiberius Kirk of the Starship Enterprise.

At every turn there's a new sight or a surprise.

A small window display dedicated to Sam Touchstone has a white bust of the man that looks a bit like Colonel Sanders of Kentucky Fried Chicken fame. There are two taxidermied frogs engaged in a boxing match (wearing boxing gloves) in a roped ring as well as other frogs in a variety of poses. Let's call these touches "eclectic" in a setting that could be interpreted as Sam Touchstone's office.

There is also a phantasmagorical faux animal that shows off Sam's taxidermy skills and his enormous sense of fun.

You just have to see the place for yourself!

GERMANTOWN COLONY MUSEUM

Vestiges of a pure Christian community on the same latitude as Jerusalem

200 Museum Road, Minden
318-377-6061
sos.la.gov
Tue–Sat 9am–4pm

Some 7 miles northeast of Minden, the Germantown Colony Museum tells the story of a small group of settlers, led by the Count and Countess von Leon, who made their way into the isolated wilderness of north Louisiana to establish a pure Christian community, their own

"kingdom of heaven." The poor count did not make it all the way, dying of yellow fever along the Red River, but his wife pushed ahead and managed to establish a remarkable settlement that endured for the next 40 years. Members of the original families still live nearby, and the site includes several original buildings and the community cemetery.

If in most accounts of Louisiana's history, the French and Spanish influence dominates, the Germans were one of the more important ethnic groups that settled the state from New Orleans to Acadiana and into the rolling hills of Webster Parish.

Three of the original buildings remain: the cabin of Countess von Leon (where we can still see a bit of the fancy wallpaper she purchased from New Orleans), a kitchen and dining hall, and the German cottage. They were all donated by the Krouse family, descendants of the original settlers.

According to Count Leon, the colony was established on the same latitude as Jerusalem as it was to be the place from which he – chosen by God – would run the world after the Second Coming of Christ. (The museum has some interesting artifacts that give a hint as to the count's religious leanings.)

Established in 1835, a year before the town of Minden was founded, the German colony lasted until 1871. The Civil War and its upheavals, and the area's economic downturn after the war, meant that it was no longer viable.

The Harmony Society

Although Count Leon founded the colony with his wife, he was also affiliated with the Harmony Society, a Christian theosophy and pietist society founded in Germany in 1785. Due to religious persecution by the Lutheran Church and the government in Württemberg, the group of approximately 400 followers moved to the United States, where they formally established the Harmony Society in 1805, holding all their goods in common.

Under its founder and spiritual leader Johann Georg Rapp (1757–1847), who was inspired by the philosophies of Jakob Böhme and Emanuel Swedenborg, among others, the Society existed for 100 years, roughly from 1805 until 1905. It is best known for the establishment of three model communities: the first at Harmony, Pennsylvania; the second, also called Harmony, in the Indiana Territory (now New Harmony, Indiana); and the third and final one in Economy (now Ambridge, Pennsylvania).

AMBUSH MUSEUM

A fascinating example of how Hollywood has mythologized Bonnie and Clyde

2419 Main Street, Gibsland
318-843-1934
Daily 9am–5pm
Admission charge

In the heart of Gibsland, a small town just off of Interstate 20, you'll find a shrine (of sorts) to the power of media to create heroes and perpetuate their myths – you can spend a couple of hours stepping back in time. The Ambush Museum is a chockablock place that could be described as an old-school roadside museum dedicated to the death of the notorious outlaws Bonnie and Clyde.

The attraction is well worth a visit, for it captures a bygone era with a 17-minute film of newsreel footage from the 1930s. The language of the commentators gives an authentic period flavor as you enter the densely populated museum.

The artifacts on display include a tam that Bonnie Parker wore that fateful day and shards of glass taken from the windshield after it was blasted apart by the lawmen who set the ambush. However, most of the larger exhibits are replicas, such as the bullet-hole-ridden car. The Ford V8 model is probably the most famous Ford out of all the millions that the company produced … and that is not an exaggeration, like the O.J Bronco of its time.

Copious newspaper clippings allow visitors to process what happened here and form their own opinions of the famous outlaws. Photos of the dead Clyde on a morgue table, a hand cast of Clyde's that was later said to be used as a family's doorstop, weapon upon weapon ... A case with the guns that Clyde had in the car when he was shot takes your breath away.

Known as the Barrow Gang or Barrow and Parker during their lifetime, the duo became forever internationally known as Bonnie and Clyde after the 1967 film starring Warren Beatty and Faye Dunaway.

The events of May 1934 and the ambush were, of course, preceded by the crime spree that became famous in the area (but not so famous nationally as the film might lead you to believe). Bonnie and Clyde killed innocent people and law enforcement officers along the way, and they mostly robbed mom-and-pop stores, so it would be hard to label them as heroes. Yet the museum is a fascinating capsule of the power of Hollywood to glorify villains.

Some 7 miles away, on Louisiana Highway 154, is a graffiti-marred monument that visitors have defaced at the exact location of the ambush.

The museum was resurrected by L.J. "Boots" Hinton in 2006 at Ma Canfield's, the diner where Bonnie and Clyde bought their last meal. (Bonnie was found with a half ham sandwich she had bought that night at the diner.) L.J. was the son of Ted Hinton, one of the six men who hunted down and killed Bonnie and Clyde on May 23, 1934. After the younger Hinton's death, Bonnie and Clyde aficionado Perry Carver has lovingly preserved the museum.

If you're interested in 20th-century American history, this spot is a goldmine where you can happily spend a couple of hours.

The replica of the shot-up car is a bit graphic, with a blood-damaged windshield and two blood-spattered mannequins representing Bonnie and Clyde in the front seats, so if you have kids with you, you might want to take that into account

DRISKILL MOUNTAIN

The highest natural summit in Louisiana

Trail entrance next to parking lot of Mount Zion Presbyterian Church
Louisiana Highway 507 in Bienville Parish, Bryceland

A primitive pyramid of rocks marks the spot: the pinnacle of Driskill Mountain at 535 ft. above sea level. Calling it a mountain is kind of a stretch, but it's the highest natural summit in Louisiana. If you ask Louisianians what the highest peak in their very flat state is, most could not name it. Now you know!

The trail that leads to Driskill Mountain – named after James Christopher Driskill, a veteran of the Civil War who bought the land in the 19th century – sits behind Mount Zion Presbyterian Church. The beginning of the trail is clearly marked. It's an easy trek, about 2 miles long, and takes about 45 minutes round trip.

After leaving your car in the church parking lot, you'll see the start of the trail clearly marked. There is a closed gate to keep out vehicles. Just walk between the gate and the post and you're on your way up a red dirt trail to your "mountain" climbing adventure.

The news is good for those who want to climb the tallest mountain in Louisiana as it's quite straightforward. Essentially, it's an uphill stroll. Anyone in good health should have no problem reaching the top.

What you'll encounter is a quiet forest trail. Approximately 15 or 20 minutes later, you'll reach the summit. There is a bench, a logbook, a bit of information, and a pile of rocks that marks the highest point in the state.

Initially, you may be underwhelmed but look for a sign on the left that alerts visitors to an overlook: In the distance, you'll see a partial view of Jordan Mountain (497 ft.), another of the Louisiana "mountains" that are actually hills.

If you reach the top of Driskill Mountain, you can brag about conquering the tallest mountain in the state; the other positive elements of a hike up Driskill are the peace and the beautiful pine forest. Chances are, if you visit in the middle of the week, you'll be the only person there.

Note that the mountain is located on private property, and it's only due to an agreement between the state and the owners that the trail is open to the public. Remember to be respectful of that fact as you hike toward the summit.

LOUISIANA POLITICAL MUSEUM & HALL OF FAME

The only political museum of its kind

499 East Main Street, Winnfield
318-628-5928
lapoliticalmuseum.com
Mon–Fri 9am–5pm

Home to the Louisiana Political Museum & Hall of Fame, the old railroad depot on Main Street in Winnfield might seem like an austere and tranquil gray wooden building from the outside. Inside, it chronicles one of the more colorful political environments in the United States.

The museum is a depository of campaign memorabilia and personal items belonging to people who were either elected officials or meandered through the colorful political history of Louisiana. Even the bathrooms are decorated with campaign flyers and posters.

The museum claims to be the only political museum of its kind … and that well may be so.

For those of you who doubt the claims of a raucous history, remember that Huey P. Long was gunned down in the Louisiana State Capitol building, that Earl Long was committed to an insane asylum while governor, and that Jimmie Davis (a gold record-winning recording artist who wrote the song "You Are My Sunshine") rode his horse up the capitol steps and into this office.

Since the opening of the museum, over 170 individuals have been inducted into the Louisiana Political Hall of Fame. The inductees include: Zachary Taylor, President of the United States; James Carville, a well-known political pundit; James Gill, a longtime journalist in New Orleans; William Jefferson, a congressman who went to prison for taking bribes; Burl Cain, warden of the infamous Louisiana State Penitentiary at Angola; Coozan Dudley LeBlanc, the huckster of all-purpose elixir Hadacol; and an assortment of legislators, sheriffs, and journalists who didn't go to jail.

The most flamboyant exhibit here is Uncle Earl's 1951 pale yellow and white Chevrolet campaign vehicle, with a high-powered speaker system attached to the top – he had three such vehicles at any given time during his campaigns. A mannequin of Earl in full stump speech pose sits next to a console with six white buttons, which allows visitors to hear his loud, distinctive campaign style.

According to the museum's director, the only criterion for inclusion in the Hall of Fame is that someone must have had a significant impact on Louisiana political life. It's a shrine to the human element in politics, that's for sure.

Huey Long and his brother Earl, known as Uncle Earl, were born in Winnfield and are the main reason that the museum and Hall of Fame are located here.

UNCLE EARL'S HOG DOG TRIALS

Louisiana's official dog breed

499 East Main Street, Winnfield
318-628-4461
jake@hogbaying.com

Around Winnfield, you may stumble upon some unusual hogs: a large, unusually decorated concrete hog, like a hog sporting a Superman leotard paint job; another hog dubbed Pigasus; and yet another that looks like it's wearing suspenders (like the former governor, Earl Kemp Long, popularly known as "Uncle Earl").

The imaginatively decorated hogs are in honor of Uncle Earl's Hog Dog Trials. This event, started in 1994, is a tribute to a cultural phenomenon in central Louisiana and a showcase for the state's official dog

breed, the Catahoula Leopard Dog (more widely known as the Catahoula cur).

The trials originated in the long tradition in this area of many families running wild hogs as an economic activity. Hogs would be released into the wild and then harvested in the spring as sustenance or to barter. They were branded on their ears, much like cattle in the Old West, with each family having its own unique brand or mark.

Specially bred for herding hogs, the Catahoula Leopard Dog is the star here. It was named the Louisiana state dog in 1979.

The Catahoula's origins are believed to be a mixing and selective breeding over time of French Beauceron dogs in the 17th century with Spanish war dogs and Native American swamp-hunting wolfdogs adapted to the rigors of the Louisiana swamp. Some historians link them to the war dogs that Desoto brought with him to Louisiana as well as dogs bred with the red wolf by Native Americans in the region.

The breed was assiduously engineered through strict breeding protocols and in the 19th century the only way to acquire a Catahoula was to be gifted one. The dogs were not sold. Even today the more serious owners who hunt them and use them as herding dogs maintain a strict attitude aimed at keeping the breed connected to its historical roots.

The Catahoula was recognized by the American Kennel Club as an American breed in 1996 after being bred over time for qualities such as work, hunting, guarding and, not least, being good with children.

Kevlar vests for dogs

Drawing over 5,000 spectators to the ring where hog dogs herd wild hogs, Uncle Earl's Hog Dog Trials are a significant event in Winnfield. Judges score many Catahoula, as well as other breeds, such as the Black Mouth Cur and the Blue Lacy, for their herding skill and tenacity.

The dogs are protected by Kevlar vests, chest armor, extra collars to prevent injury. Ther hogs are released into the wild once the trophies are awarded.

The name Catahoula comes from the Choctaw nation and means "sacred lake."

GRAVE OF A MARRIED MAN

An amazing story from another century

Old City Cemetery, Monroe
Elysian Fields Road
At the intersection of 9th Street, Desiard Street, and Elysian Fields Road
findagrave.com/memorial/7142941/sidney-w-saunders

n downtown Monroe, in the Old City Cemetery, the statue of a stately gentleman may look like many other monuments, but this one stands out because of what is carved on the marble document prominently displayed in his hand. The back story reveals the social mores of another century.

This is the grave known as the Grave of a Married Man. Sidney Saunders was his name and Annie Livingston was his wife.

Saunders was a successful yet controversial businessman in Monroe circa 1870–1889. He ran a popular grocery store and had other businesses such as a flourishing saloon. It seems that during his heyday, he went on a trip and returned with, as the gossip put it, "a wife on his arm."

When the couple returned after marrying in St. Louis, they had a one-year-old son Willie in tow. Willie died at the age of 12, which adds a sad touch to the saga.

Saunders later had troubles and enjoyed poor standing in the community. This seems to have originated in the fact that a fire raced up to the second floor of his saloon and ended up burning down a good part of downtown Monroe. Subsequent fires at other buildings owned by Saunders led to mass speculation that he was an arsonist.

During his trial for arson, Saunders purchased a lot in the Monroe City Cemetery. About ten days later, his wife came out of the house screaming as Sidney had been found with a bullet wound at the back of his head. The death was ruled a suicide.

Mrs. Saunders, who had bristled under the rumors that they were never legally married, had the marriage certificate put in Saunders's hand on his grave, where he still holds it today.

The 1880 Ouachita Parish census lists Saunders as single and Annie Livingston as residing at another address. However, Annie acquired a certified registry of the marriage from St. Louis – it is on display today at the Ouachita Parish Library.

Annie is said to have kept her husband's body in a shed behind her home until the tomb was ready.

There was a 10-ft.-square room where Annie would sit in a rocking chair and sew all day while speaking with visitors beside the three caskets for Sidney, Willie, and herself. She kept Sidney's desk and Willie's velocipede in the room.

CHENNAULT AVIATION & MILITARY MUSEUM

In memory of the leader of the Chinese Air Force

701 Kansas Lane, Monroe
318-362-5540
chennaultmuseum.org
Tue–Sat 9am–4pm

Housed in the remnants of Selman Field, which served as the chief school for flight navigators during World War II, the General Claire Chennault Museum is a depository of American military history with many interesting exhibits that focus on the individual soldier. Uniforms, weapons, utensils of everyday life in a war zone, personal effects and photos can be examined in numerous cases chock-full of memorabilia.

The airpark is also a treat for military buffs as you can walk right up to famous machines like a *P-40 Warhawk* fighter, nose painted with a ferocious facial expression and mounted high in a tilted pose as if about to perform a dive to engage the enemy.

Also on display are the *F-86 Sabre*, a Korean War-era fighter known for its efficiency and speed; an *MR-18 Light Bomber*, which Chennault

pilots used to ferry materials into China; and *MiG-15*, which became the standard Communist bloc fighter during the Cold War.

Chennault, who became one of America's most celebrated military personalities, was raised in nearby Gilbert. After becoming a pilot in World War II, he had mixed success in his military career. His fame grew after he became leader of the Chinese Air Force: The Chinese were particularly keen on Chennault because of his innovative approach to aeronautics, which they thought suited their need to counter a vastly superior Japanese air force.

Chennault jumped at the chance. He resigned from the U.S. Army and went to China, eventually becoming the leader of the American Volunteer Group, where he recruited American pilots to fight for China. This group became better known as the Flying Tigers, one of the most famous American fighting units in World War II.

The Selman Field Navigation School was the largest navigation school in the U.S. during World War II. A soldier could enter Selman, complete his training, and leave as a Second Lieutenant. Fifteen thousand navigators trained at Selman during World War II.

BIBLE MUSEUM

One of the finest Bible collections in the world

2000 Riverside Drive, Monroe
318-387-581
bmuseum.org
Tue–Sat 10am–5pm

Tucked away between the Biedenharn Coca-Cola Museum and the Biedenharn Mansion on the banks of the Ouachita River in Monroe, the Bible Museum is an unexpected repository of antique Bibles. The collection is one of the finest in the country and is thanks to Emma-Louise Biedenharn (1902–84), the only daughter of Joseph Biedenharn, the first bottler of Coca-Cola and a successful confectioner from Vicksburg, Mississippi. (His candy store is still in operation in downtown Vicksburg.)

Joseph also co-founded Delta Airlines and his family went on to become philanthropists and generous patrons of the arts in northeastern Louisiana after they made their home in Monroe.

Emmy-Lou's Bible collection began because of a gift from her father: an 1854 facsimile of the Wycliffe Bible. This led her to compile what is now one of the most important collections of Bibles in the world and a well-known resource for biblical scholars.

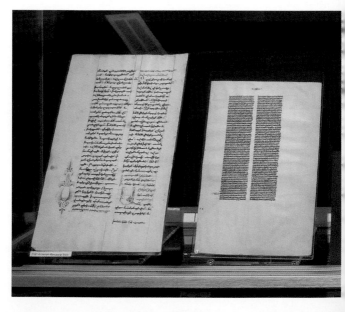

The collection includes many exciting and historical Bibles, such as a page from the 1454–55 Gutenberg Bible, an original 1611 St. James Bible, an Armenian manuscript Bible (1121), a Rusch Bible (1480), an Aldine Greek Bible (1518), a Julia Smith Bible (1640; the first Bible ever translated by women), the 1640 Bay Psalm Book (believed to be

the first book ever printed in what would eventually become the United States), and three pages from a Bible translated into the Algonquin language.

Emmy-Lou was the daughter of wealth, as is evident from her Bible collection, the immaculate grounds and her residence and eclectic furnishings, which can all be seen on the tours.

Emmy-Lou: a fairytale life

Emmy-Lou lived a fairytale life. Trained early as a singer and musician, she left for Europe after a brief stint at DePauw University. Under the tutelage in London of Sir George Henschel, the recognized operatic guru of his time, she became the toast of European opera houses as one of the greatest operatic voices of the era. At 6 ft. 4 in. tall and weighing 300 lb., she was quite the stereotypical operatic presence. Said to be good-natured and quick to laughter, she was very popular. She sang all over Europe in a career that lasted 14 years. Emmy-Lou was living in Denmark, the Biedenharns' ancestral home, when Germany invaded Poland in 1939. She returned to Monroe and became a generous contributor to the community. Her influence on the arts did not end with her European career, as her fame lured celebrated musicians and singers to Monroe to perform in her gardens. Her rendition of "God Bless America" could move people to tears.

The Gun-Wad Bible

The museum also has pages from what is known as the Gun-Wad Bible, dating from the Revolutionary War era (1775–83): It was cannibalized so its pages could be torn apart and used as gun wadding for muskets.

TOMB OF UNALASKA

The lead sled dog of Admiral Byrd's 1929 expedition to the South Pole

Georgia Tucker Elementary School
405 Stubbs Avenue, Monroe
Outside the gardens at Georgia Tucker
318-538-0040
georgiatucker.com

Outside the gardens at Georgia Tucker (an assisted living facility that opened in 2018 in a once-cherished public school), a weathered marble headstone below two white columns reminds us of the remarkable story of Unalaska, the lead sled dog of Admiral Richard Byrd's 1929 expedition to the South Pole.

A symphony of diversity – part Irish Setter, St. Bernard, Siberian Husky and wolf – Unalaska was said to have been handpicked for the expedition by Byrd himself. He performed heroically in his task of leading the sled teams in the unforgiving conditions at the South Pole.

After Byrd's triumphant South Pole expedition, the adventurer toured the United States, taking Unalaska with him. By many accounts, the dog was the star of the tour, especially with children.

On the Monroe leg of the tour, Unalaska was taken for exercise in a local park but on the way back to the school (where he was appearing along with the admiral), he was struck and killed by a hit-and-run driver who was never identified. The city of Monroe and its schoolchildren went into mourning. At the suggestion of the school principal, Julia Wossman, the children were put in charge of the funeral, which was reported in newspapers all over the nation.

With the permission of the city of Monroe, Unalaska was buried in Forsyth Park in the American Legion cemetery between two French artillery cannons that had fought in World War I. He was laid to rest in a white velvet casket lined with pink satin. A construction company donated a 700-lb. piece of Indiana granite and a bronze plaque with Unalaska's exploits inscribed on the monument.

Two thousand children marched in the funeral procession. There was a Boy Scouts honor guard, the American Legion Home lowered the flag to half-staff, and thousands of citizens walked by the casket to pay their respects to the fallen hero.

All seemed to be in order until the following day when, amazingly, it was discovered that the monument to Unalaska was gone and the 700-lb. piece of stone had been stolen. The theft stunned the community and the monument was never recovered.

The schoolchildren of Monroe were still determined to honor their new hero: They collected pennies and nickels to rebury Unalaska in the grounds of Georgia Tucker Elementary School, where the sled dog still rests today.

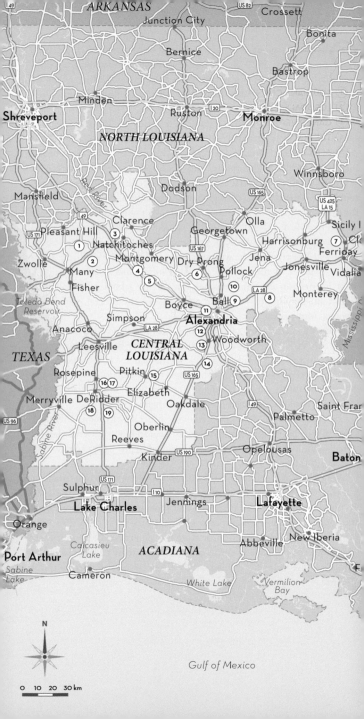

Central Louisiana

LOUISIANA COUNTRY MUSIC HALL OF FAME

An excellent introduction to the greats of country music

Rebel State Park, 1260 Highway 1221, Marthaville
318-472-6255 – 888-677-3600
lastateparks.com/historic-sites/rebel-state-historic-site – rebelmgr@crt.la.gov
Museum: Fri & Sat 9am–5pm. Grounds: Thurs–Sat 9am–5pm
Admission charge

Just outside Marthaville in northwestern Louisiana, the Louisiana Country Music Hall of Fame, although small, is a modern museum that provides an excellent introduction to the genre and to the Louisiana

natives who made a significant contribution to this essential American music. Although Jimmie Davis and Jerry Lee Lewis are given special consideration, many other artists are honored, from Johnny Cash (who had Louisiana connections) to some of the country music greats who all played on a live radio show called the Louisiana Hayride.

Several rooms survey the history of country and western music. From the importance of musical traditions in church to the secular honky-tonks, there are exhibits that touch on every aspect of the importance of country music. Artifacts associated with the stars include: Johnny Cash's shirt, Ernest Tubb's hat and shirt, Roy Acuff's fiddle and yo-yo, George Jones's shirt, and Grandpa Jones's cowbell. Many of the items were signed and donated by the musicians themselves. Also on display are Cathedral Radios, old Victrolas and even a 1910 Edison recording machine in tribute to the inventions that spread country music far and wide.

One of the museum's sweeter features is the Musical Petting Zoo. It's a display of instruments, including a guitar, a banjo, a zither, a tambourine, and maracas, that visitors, especially children, are encouraged to pick up and play. The sign says, 'Be gentle, just like at a real petting zoo.'

The Louisiana Hayride

Prominently honored here in Marthaville, the Louisiana Hayride has a special place in country and rockabilly history. Less famous than the Grand Ole Opry in Nashville, it gave unknown stars exposure and helped nurture their careers. In so doing, it gave many of the biggest stars in the business their start. The familiar opening lines of the Hayride broadcast (from a song by the Bailes Brothers and Red Sovine) are displayed on a wall in the museum: 'Come along, come along. The sun is shining bright, the moon is shining bright. We're gonna have a Louisiana Hayride tonight.'

Just outside the museum is a nicely sized outdoor amphitheater designed to accommodate hundreds of fans for concerts and events like the Louisiana State Fiddle Championship. Sadly, the theater has not been used for a show since 2006.

The name *Louisiana Hayride* was the title of a 1941 book by Harnett Thomas Kane, *Louisiana Hayride: The American Rehearsal for Dictatorship*, a critical examination of Huey Long's autocratic rise to power as governor and U.S. senator and the cabal that seized his mantle after his assassination in 1935. It was also the name of a song in the 1932 Broadway musical *Flying Colors*.

LOS ADAES

The former capital of the province of Texas

6354 Louisiana Highway 485, Robeline
318-356-5555
lastateparks.com/historic-sites/los-adaes-state-historic-site
Wed–Sat noon–4pm

t's a hard-to-believe and little-known fact: The very seat and saddle of Texas, indeed the actual capital city of the Lone Star State, once stood near what is today Robeline, Louisiana.

A mere 13 miles west of Natchitoches, a mission called Presidio Nuestra Señora del Pilar de Los Adaes (Fort of Our Lady of Pilar at the Adaes), symbol of New Spain in Louisiana, was designated in 1729 by Spain as the capital of the province of Texas. (The name Adaes is derived from the indigenous Adai tribe.) This made Los Adaes not only the capital of Texas but also the official residence of its governor: A house was constructed for him within a fort surrounded by a hexagonal stockade with three bulwarks.

Today, a small Louisiana State Park rests on this quiet site in the pine woods. While unfortunately no original buildings remain, timbers have been used to create an outline of the hexagonal fort so that visitors may see the original size and layout of the structures that once stood at Los Adaes. This place, deep in the lush Louisiana woods, is also considered one of the most significant archeological sites for the study of Spanish colonial culture. An informative interpretive center tells the unique history of this area, where Spanish, French, American and indigenous people came into contact and forged a unique mix that developed into a distinctive culture.

The origins of Los Adaes are interesting. In 1714, the French founded Natchitoches with the establishment of Fort St. Jean Baptiste. The Spanish, fearing encroachment on their territory in Texas, soon decided to establish a series of missions in the area. After raids on these missions by French forces, the Spanish Crown decided to build a fort at this site.

Los Adaes thrived and remained the administrative seat of government for the entire province until 1770 (ten years after Louisiana was transferred to Spain). However, it was abandoned in 1770, when the Texas capital was moved to San Antonio. Even though roughly 500 soldiers and their families left Los Adaes for San Antonio at the time, historians believe that many soon returned to the Los Adaes area, where some of their descendants still remain.

The Camino Real de Tejas (the 'royal road' that led to Mexico City) began here and provided the main land route for French, Spanish, and American settlers to travel to Mexico City. After Los Adaes was abandoned, the Camino Real remained a vital trade route from Louisiana to Mexico. During the Civil War, the Confederate States used the route to circumvent Union blockades.

In downtown Natchitoches there is a reconstructed Fort St. Jean Baptiste.

CANE RIVER FOSSILS

One of the most important paleontology sites in Louisiana

Southbound lane following Exit 148, Natchitoches
Abandoned exit ramp on Interstate 49

Near Natchitoches, the oldest town in Louisiana on Interstate 49, about an hour south of Shreveport in the southbound lane, you'll see an abandoned exit ramp that was once destined to be used as a rest stop. If you pull over onto the unfinished exit and park your car, you can wander towards a raised area designed as the ramp to the abandoned rest stop. It creates a berm-like wall overlooking a ditch.

On the side of the wall of raised soil, you can see evidence of a once-shallow ocean with a similar terrain and depth to today's Gulf of Mexico. The outcropping turns out to be a neat place to see and collect fossils that are up to 46 million years old.

The site is considered one of the most important paleontology sites in Louisiana and has more than one name: Middle Eocene Cane River Formation, Cane River Site or the I-49 site. It is considered the best exposure of Cane River Formation in the state.

The formation reaches into Natchitoches, but in the city the fossils are hard to access due to the trappings of civilization, namely concrete and buildings. Here, on the side of the interstate, you can actually see and touch the fossils.

This part of Louisiana was once under water and part of what would become the Gulf of Mexico. Consequently, you can find a proliferation of maritime creatures such as bivalves, coral, shark teeth, and numerous microscopic fossils: Over 150 species of marine fossils (called ostracods) have been found here.

It's a strange spot to gather shells up here in northwestern Louisiana on the side of Interstate 49 as cars speed by, but it's also quite unique.

THE PORCH OF P. PHANOR PRUDHOMME GENERAL STORE

One of the least-known "battles" of World War II

4386 Louisiana Highway 119, Natchez

t was from the porch of the restored but now closed general store of P. Phanor Prudhomme, within easy viewing distance of the so-called Bermuda Bridge, that one of the least-known "battles" of World War II started.

What some have dubbed the "Battle of Bermuda Bridge" occurred on September 26, 1941. That day, the United States Army had assembled up to 450,000 men to modernize the tactics and test the equipment that would wage and eventually win what would be known as World War II: The Blue Army and the Red Army would hold wargames around the Cane River.

From P. Phanor Prudhomme's store, siblings Alphonse, Mayo, and Ken observed a soldier of the Blue Army across the river in what was then thick foliage. As most young boys of the time (they were 14, 12

and 9 respectively), they were fascinated by the military. They were also armed with a healthy dose of mischief and a "Big Bang Cannon," a small carbide cannon they had received as a gift. The boys decided to fire the cannon, making a very loud noise. Startled by the report, the soldier fell out of the tree and drove hastily off.

Within a few minutes, the Blue Army forces arrived and furiously opened fire with blanks at what they thought was the Red Army. The boys continued to fire in earnest at the forces of the U.S. Army. They were having the time of their lives.

Their father, Alphonse Prudhomme, then entered the fray. He gave his hired hand a bunch of firecrackers and the boys then escalated the fray. So, for 15 to 30 minutes, the Prudhomme boys and the U.S. Army had a faux shootout. Loud bangs, accompanied by the smoke created by the guns and firecrackers, added to the authentic feel of a war game.

At some point, the military umpires figured out what was going on and approached Mr. Prudhomme with this request. "Would you mind calling your boys off so we could get on with our war?"

So ended the Battle of Bermuda Bridge.

In 1989 Kenneth Prudhomme got a call from a friend telling him to tune in to the radio. Only then did he realize that the army he had "defeated" (or at least sent on the run) that day in 1941 was the 2nd Armored Division commanded by General George S. Patton.

AFRICAN HOUSE

Congo-style architecture

Melrose Plantation
3533 Louisiana Highway 119
318-379-0055
melroseplantation.org
spacesrarchives.org/explore/search-the-online-collection/clementine-hunter-
melrose-plantation
Thurs–Sun 10am–3pm
Admission charge

Sitting at the back of the big house at Melrose Plantation (Melrose on the Cane), African House claims to be the only structure in the United States to be conceived, designed, and built by and for people of African descent in what is believed to be a Congo-style architecture.

Melrose itself was built around 1800 (dates vary) by a free family of color and, as such, is one of the oldest plantations constructed by and for African Americans.

It was started by Louis Metoyer, whose mother, Marie Thérèse Coincoin, was enslaved. After her freedom was purchased, she became a wealthy businesswoman: The family was rich and free for four generations before the Civil War.

African House (which has recently been renovated) is constructed of large slave-made bricks, heavy-hewn timber, highly mortised, which means it used no nails to connect and secure the elements it was built

with. A hip roof of cypress shingles and a 12-ft. overhang give it a distinctive Congo look.

There are no records concerning the building's construction, and consequently, its origins have led to much speculation.

Over the years, it has been used for various purposes, notably as a storehouse and an artist's residency. The latter led to one of its best-known claims to fame – its association with the renowned American folk artist, Clementine Hunter.

A true hero and a legend

Clementine Hunter's work is found on the second floor of the building in the murals depicting life on the plantation. Her story is compelling. Melrose's role granting residencies to artists led to Hunter's being discovered. One of the visiting artists, Francois Mignon, encouraged her to paint after she had presented him with one of her works. At the time, she was a cook at Melrose. She had lived there since the age of 12 and had worked the cotton fields: Her work portrays the ebb and flow of life on a Cane River plantation. Over four decades of painting in what is known as the American Primitive style, Hunter became a famous artist. She produced between 5,000 and 10,000 paintings, and although she sold some for as little as 25 cents, they now go for thousands of dollars and hang in some of the finest museums in the United States. Hunter's most famous work (the African House Murals), created when she was 68, is still at Melrose on the second floor of the house – the series is painted with oils on plywood and depicts life on Melrose Plantation. The murals were removed in 2005, painstakingly restored and placed back on the second story. They can now be seen by visitors to the property.

COLFAX MASSACRE MEMORIAL

The worst case of racial violence during the Reconstruction era

Louisiana Highway 158 along railroad tracks one block from intersection of Louisiana Highway 8
Alexandria–Colfax Highway, Colfax

I n the center of Colfax, along the railroad tracks in a prominent site alongside buildings that are the site of the annual Pecan Festival, stands a sobering 7-ft. granite monument. It is a reminder of an event during the turbulent Reconstruction era (1861–1900) that had enormous consequences for African American voting rights.

The memorial bears the name of 57 African American citizens who were killed in what is now known as the Colfax Massacre (April 13, 1873) and boasts artwork by artist Jazzmen Lee-Johnson commemorating these violent events. The monument was erected in April 2023 after a community effort backed by descendants of both white and African American survivors of the event, with $65,000 donations raised from various sources.

Historians consider the Colfax Massacre to be the worst case of racial violence during the Reconstruction period. A disputed election result in 1872 caused widespread conflict in Louisiana, as had almost every election in the South since the end of the Civil War.

During this time in Louisiana, the disputed elections and jockeying for elective power led to many armed conflicts, including one in which 8,000 armed men favoring the Democratic candidates descended on New Orleans to fight 3,500 Republican supporters. Federal troops eventually had to be brought in to end the conflict.

Events in Colfax that led to the massacre were set in motion when an African American farmer was murdered in front of his family while tending his field. Local African Americans fled to the courthouse and started to fortify it by digging trenches. Local white citizens (many of them former Confederate soldiers) surrounded the courthouse and demanded its surrender. After the women and children had been allowed to leave, the story starts to differ depending upon who is telling the tale.

The whites claim that one of the African American men fired and shot one of the whites in violation of the truce that had been agreed on. The African American witnesses deny this. What followed was a systematic slaughter of African American citizens: Estimates of the number killed range from 57 to 153.

The story of the massacre reached the wider American audience through press reports. The federal government sent troops and indicted some of the white men involved, invoking the Enforcement Act of 1870 which was implemented by Congress to enforce the 14th Amendment. Some of the men were convicted but a Supreme Court judge presiding over the trial freed them after ruling that the 1870 Enforcement Act did not apply.

For all practical purposes, this ruling ended the Enforcement Act and led to a growing movement in the South to disenfranchise African Americans.

In 1951, another historical marker (calling the event the Colfax Riot) was erected at the courthouse. It was torn down in 2021.

DELTA MUSIC MUSEUM

A gem of a music museum

218 Louisiana Avenue, Ferriday
318-757-9999
deltamusicmuseum.com
friends@deltamusicmuseum.com
Wed–Fri 9am–4pm

In a quite sturdy former post office in the heart of downtown Ferriday, the Delta Music Museum – the only Louisiana site on the Delta Blues Trail – is an extremely well-presented gem of a place dedicated to some of Louisiana's most famous musicians … and a little bit more.

On arrival, you'll be warmly greeted by docents who are more than happy to tell you about the exhibits and answer any questions you may have.

The main attraction is, of course, the three famous musical cousins who called Ferriday home: Mickey Gilley, Jimmy Swaggart, and Jerry Lee Lewis. The museum has several of their personal items that were donated by the community, as was the building, which was gifted by a local benefactor.

Exhibits donated by Ferriday's three sons greet you as you enter the space to the left. It is touching to see the teenage and childhood photos of the trio.

But there is much more to see than the three famous sons, as the museum showcases a wide variety of Louisiana musical stars. All genres are represented here, with New Orleans musical stars like Irma Thomas, Clarence 'Frogman' Henry, Pete Fountain, and an important member of the musical pantheon, Allen 'Puddler' Harris. Harris, who is less known in the outside world, was born in Jigger. He had quite a career as a member of the Twitty Birds, who backed up the country star, and was also a member of Ricky Nelson's band in Hollywood.

A short film pays tribute to another native son of Ferriday: broadcasting legend, Howard K. Smith.

More number-one hits than Frank Sinatra, The Beatles or Elvis Presley …

The Twitty exhibit in the museum points out that Conway Twitty, who went to high school not that far away in Tallulah, had more number-one hits in the charts than Frank Sinatra, The Beatles or Elvis Presley.

NEARBY
The childhood home of Jerry Lee Lewis

Five blocks from the museum, at 712 Louisiana Avenue, next to a drive-through beer barn, is the childhood home of Jerry Lee Lewis. The house was formerly a museum but sadly was closed in 2023.

LOUISIANA MANEUVERS AND MILITARY MUSEUM

The largest military operation of its kind in U.S. history

Camp Beauregard
623 G. Street, Pineville
318-641-5733
geauxguardmuseums.com
Tue–Fri 9am–5pm

Hidden inside Camp Beauregard, a working army base, the Louisiana Maneuvers and Military Museum is a beautifully presented exhibit of American military history and gives a unique insight into one of the most forgotten contributions to the United States' victory in World War II.

Two unique exhibits showcase the home front, with artifacts of everyday life in the U.S. such as ration cards and the story of the 761st

Tank Battalion, the first African American tank unit in the U.S. Army. The 761st's exploits during the war, much like the more famous Tuskegee Airmen, made an important contribution towards changing attitudes in the army hierarchy and led to the segregation of the U.S. Armed Forces in 1948 – they are an aspect of U.S. military history that frequently flies under the radar.

Visitor is greeted by an imposing *UH-1 Iroquois* helicopter, an iconic symbol of the Vietnam War, hovering poised in midair as if ready for action.

A vehicle park beyond the working latrines provided for visitors has tanks, artillery, armored vehicles and other military hardware that is a treat for any military buff to examine up close.

Inside the museum, exhibits provide a survey of U.S. military history from the Revolutionary War to the Gulf War with documents, photos, newspaper articles, flags, and military paraphernalia such as PPSh-41 submachine guns used by the North Korean and Chinese troops in the Korean War, as well as swords and other vintage weapons, and uniforms from the Civil War and various other conflicts.

One of the exhibits showcases the testing and ultimate approval of the C-ration (a military ration consisting of prepared, canned wet foods) here in Louisiana.

The star attraction, though, is the chronicle of the Louisiana Maneuvers, an under-appreciated but monumental training exercise held by the U.S. Army from August to September of 1941 in a vast area of central and north Louisiana. As war loomed in Europe, Army chief of staff George C. Marshall chose Louisiana as an experimental training ground after sending General Lesley McNair and General Mark Clark on a fact-finding mission to the state. They found that central Louisiana was just what was needed to test new strategies and equipment.

On September 15, 1941, a mock battle with as many as 472,000 soldiers and 50,000 military vehicles was held to test modern strategies for waging war. That exercise was the largest military operation of its kind in U.S. history.

Junior officer Dwight D. Eisenhower, who was appointed Lieutenant General Walter Krueger's chief of staff for the exercise, emerged as a rising star during the Louisiana Maneuvers. General George C. Patton also gained a distinguished reputation here in Louisiana.

OLD LSU SITE

The birthplace of a great university

Kisatchie National Forest
2000 Shreveport Highway, Pineville

Just north of Alexandria in Pineville, inside the Kisatchie Nation-al Forest, a few piles of bricks are all that remains of the original buildings of LSU, the flagship university of Louisiana, which moved to its present site at Baton Rouge after the Civil War. A pine-tree-shroud-ed paved walkway with intermittent kiosks gives information on the founding of LSU at this very spot. This out-of-the-way historical site also provides a pleasant and informative walk on a serpentine sidewalk. Benches and picnic tables are provided. The reason for the Pineville location was, among other things, that the governor of Louisiana, James Madison Wells, and George Mason Graham, the president of the Board of Trustees for the fledgling university, were both from Rapides Parish.

Building started in 1859 and the Seminary of Learning in the State of Louisiana, with 5 professors and 19 students, opened on January 2, 1860. These were roiling times in the history of the United States in the lead-up to the Civil War, and the new university was not immune to the national mood. Military education was at the forefront of the curricu-lum, and the students (all male) were more aptly called cadets.

The university's first superintendent was a retired U.S. general, Wil-liam Tecumseh Sherman. LSU's nickname (still in use today) is "The

Ole War Skule," an indication of its military background. Sherman, who would go on to fame (or infamy, depending upon your viewpoint) in the "War Between the States," resigned as superintendent as soon as Louisiana seceded from the Union.

The school closed after only one year due to the uncertainty caused by the outbreak of war, and because most students resigned after the secession to join the Confederate army. It reopened in 1862 but closed once again due to the invasion of the Red River area by Union forces under General Nathaniel Banks.

After the war the university reopened in 1865, but its presence in Pineville was short-lived as in 1869 it burned down. Ironically, it was rebuilt at the urging of General Sherman, who is forever known as the man who burned down Atlanta and a great deal of Georgia during the Civil War. In 1870, the school moved to Baton Rouge, where its name was eventually changed to Louisiana State University.

NEARBY
The marrying swing ⑩
Louisiana Christian University, 1140 College Drive, Pineville
In front of Cottingham Hall
318-487-7000 – lcuniversity.edu

In front of Cottingham Hall at Louisiana Christian University, an orange wooden swing looks just like any old swing built to accommodate two people comfortably. But according to school lore, this swing has magical powers. Once upon a time – a simpler time – many colleges and universities had campus traditions that lent a sweetness to college life. This swing and its backstory harken back to that time. It is believed that if sweethearts sit on this swing together, they will marry. Alas, the swing in front of Cottingham Hall is not the original one, which was damaged in 2010–11 (all the swings on campus were replaced in 2015), but it's the thought that counts. If you ask someone on campus who knows the tradition, they will tell you the swing nearest to Cottingham is the one. Louisiana Christian University (formerly Louisiana College) is a picture-perfect college campus that could be taken from central casting. Cottingham Hall, the women's dorm, is also the site of the "rolling of Cottingham Forest." Every year, there is a Mom's Day when female students and their mothers spend time together on campus. Yet another tradition says that rubbing the head of a statue of Moses in front of the Weathersby Fine Arts Building will bring you good luck.

HOTEL BENTLEY ATRIUM

A splendid atrium, little known outside Alexandria

200 Desoto Street, Alexandria
318-442-2226
visithotelbentley.com

Although the gorgeous atrium of the Hotel Bentley is not a secret in Alexandria itself, it is surprisingly very little known in the rest of Louisiana. Built in 1908 by a timber baron after he was refused service at a restaurant in another Alexandria hotel, the Bentley takes up a whole block of Desoto Street in downtown Alexandria. Renovated in 2012, its splendid atrium is an epitome of elegance that once led to it being called the chief jewel of central Louisiana.

Joseph Bentley spent $700,000 to build this opulent hotel, which he hoped would rival anything in New Orleans or Shreveport. To that end, he hired George R. Mann of Little Rock who had worked in New York City for McKim, Mead & White, recognized as the most influential design firm in the United States. The result is a classic Renaissance-style hotel in central Louisiana which can still wow visitors today.

Bentley lived at the hotel until his death in 1939. It was closed in 2004 and bought by Michael Jenkins, who renovated it and reopened it in 2012.

The most striking parts of the exterior are the seven two-story Ionic columns that rise to a veranda with rocking chairs that allow you to while away an afternoon with a book or a cocktail.

The most compelling vision of the Hotel Bentley remains the atrium, with a shallow dome, an oculus and a double staircase rising to a mezzanine from which you can observe the movement of the crowd below. The atrium is adorned by ornamental plaster and scrolled moldings bordering the ceiling.

The dome, which is not visible from the exterior, originally sported a fancy motif by a Romanian artist. It was repainted sometime in the 1990s by New Orleans artist Nicholas Crowell with a more pastoral scene. The effect of the architectural motifs, blue dome, chandeliers and fancy tiled floors is spectacular and quite an unexpected sight.

The Bentley was planned to exude luxury – the architect George R. Mann's design, which is reminiscent of mansions in the East, does not disappoint on that count. The Mirror Room, an Art Nouveau/Art Deco bar in the basement, adds an elegant touch to the vintage atmosphere.

Mann also designed the Fordyce Bathhouse in Hot Springs, Arkansas, when Hot Springs was at the zenith of its reputation as a resort.

A World War II exhibit

Dwight Eisenhower, George S. Patton, Omar Bradley and Joseph Stilwell stayed at the hotel and there is a small World War II exhibit on the first mezzanine near to the elevators.

BLUE TILE IN BENTLEY HOTEL ATRIUM

An imperfection as recognition that only God can create perfection

200 Desoto Street, Alexandria
318-442-2226
visithotelbentley.com

Hidden in plain sight among the thousands of tiles in the 10,000-sq.-ft floor of the elegant mosaic below the Bentley Hotel atrium, you'll find what is thought to be a signature of the artist/craftsperson who laid the tiles. It can take a while to find it unless someone points it out.

Among a palette that includes red, green, ivory, black, and gold hexagonal tiles, you'll find only one blue tile. One can imagine the artist's sense of pride and fun running through the tiles and thinking that even 100 years after this blue dot was set here, people might share a sense of joy by searching for it.

Joseph Bentley wanted to use as many local and American materials as possible in his hotel, and the foundation relies on limestone from the Red River. However, he still needed to import Italian marble to supply much of the sense of luxury that lives on today.

The one-off blue dot in the Bentley floor mosaic also points to an almost universal human custom practiced by artists of many cultures: incorporating an imperfection in their art as recognition that only God or nature can create perfection.

This custom is common to almost every culture. It is found prominently in Islamic art. The Navajo add imperfections to their designs called *ch'ihónít'i*, or spirit lines. Hagi pottery of Japan has built-in flaws, and even European craftsmen would add imperfections to buildings. Intentional flaws can also be found in some architectural designs: for example, in the National Cathedral in Washington, DC (when walking toward the altar down the main aisle, you must take a slightly left course to see the altar because the Great Choir area is slightly off axis to the rest of the design).

EDWIN EPPS HOUSE

The original location of Twelve Years a Slave

Solomon Northup Gateway to Freedom Museum
8100 Louisiana Highway 71 South, LSU Alexandria
318-473-6417 – cenlafocus.com/the-epps-house-at-lsua
Thurs–Sun noon–4pm

Built in 1852, the simple one-story Creole cottage sitting in a large grass lot on the campus of LSU Alexandria has quite a story to tell. Just a short drive on Interstate 49 south of Alexandria, the house is known as the Edwin Epps House, after its original owner. The cottage is the one that Solomon Northup (see opposite) helped build when he was a slave, as told in the book-turned-movie, *Twelve Years a Slave*.

Thanks to LSU Alexandria historian Dr. Sue Eakin, the cottage was moved to the Alexandria campus in 1999 and now houses the Solomon Northup Gateway to Freedom Museum. Its mission is to bring the story of plantation life into focus, using the narrative of Northup's life as a guide.

Today, the house has a room covering Northup's life story and other rooms dedicated to plantation life, with an emphasis on the inhumanity of slavery.

Solomon Northup: the free man of color who wrote Twelve Years a Slave

Born in 1808 as a free person in New York, Solomon Northup was a farmer and violinist. When performing one day in Washington, D.C., where slavery was still legal in 1853, he was drugged and unlawfully kidnapped and sold at Washington's slave market. He was sold again in New Orleans to Edwin Epps, and for twelve years was enslaved in Avoyelles Parish. A few years later, Epps hired the carpenter Samuel Bass to build the house that now sits at LSU Alexandria. While building the house with Bass, Northup told him his story. Bass then contacted New York about Northup's circumstances: New York State had laws that helped to free people of color who had been kidnapped. Northup returned to New York, became a popular lecturer on the issue of abolition after regaining his freedom and penned a best-selling autobiography, *Twelve Years a Slave*, issued by the same publisher as *Uncle Tom's Cabin*. It sold over 30,000 copies and was made into an Academy-Award-winning film in 2013.

SOUTHERN FOREST HERITAGE MUSEUM

Timber for the boats that landed in France on D-Day

77 Longleaf Road, Longleaf
318-748-8404
forestheritagemuseum.org
Wed–Sat 9am–4pm
Admission charge

Hidden in the rich forestland of central Louisiana, the Southern Forest Heritage Museum is housed in beautiful old buildings that retain the remnants of a once-thriving sawmill. The rustic setting and the weathered look of the museum, the authentic feel of the attraction, the buildings, the vintage equipment and the overall content all make for a fascinating day trip.

The commissary still looks like it did back in the day, and there are lots of exhibits about the sawmill industry and the forestry business.

A short video explains the importance of Louisiana forestry not only to the state economy but also to the national and even world economies. As you delve into the history of Louisiana, especially from the late 1880s to the early 20th century, you will realize the enormous economic importance of timber, and this spot deep in the woods is a great place to learn about that once-flourishing industry.

The most exciting and striking elements, though, are the outbuildings.

The Machine Shop still functions and shows how a single central shaft powered the multiple heavy milling machines using belts. The power plant had three large boilers to provide steam power for a Corliss engine that rotated the 120-ft. shaft from under the mill.

A roundhouse, a mill reserve pond where the logs were stored, a sawmill with large high smokestacks, two dry kiln buildings, two large lumber storage buildings that you may drive your car through, a planer mill, and various outbuildings where you can walk among the equipment all make you wonder what this place must once have looked like.

The link between this enterprise and the mill's contribution to winning World War II is showcased, including the fact that the sawmill here at Longleaf was the largest supplier of specialized timber used in the keels of the Higgins Boats. Designed and built in New Orleans by Andrew Higgins, the Higgins boats were instrumental in the landings at D-Day and later in the vicious island-to-island campaign in the Pacific Theater.

TALBERT-PIERSON CEMETERY

Unusual graves surrounded by wooden enclosures

825 Victor Martin Road, Vernon Parish (nr. Pitkin)
The cemetery is behind Pine Grove Methodist Church

In a remote area of Vernon Parish, down a side road behind Pine Grove Methodist Church on the appropriately named Talbert-Pierson Road, you'll find the unusual sight of graves surrounded by wooden enclosures.

The grave houses are primarily wooden, originally made from hand-split wood. They have evolved into open-air, shed-like structures. Many are surrounded by picket fences. True to the cemetery's name, many of the graves are marked as belonging to Talberts or Piersons.

The graves, which were constructed between 1889 and 1948, are a mystery: Historians still speculate on the whys and wherefores of their existence. Historians credit the Upland southern tradition of covering

graves with wooden structures to prevent them being desecrated by wild animals. The gravestones have a 'melting-pot' creation story, bringing together southern Protestant and Native American traditions: Many graves and houses are adorned with shells, including cowrie shells, which give an African feeling. Europeans introduced burial traditions such as cairns or rock coverings, wrought-iron shields to protect the graves, rock slabs known as 'wolf stones', and low-set roofs with colorful anime hog-back tombs. Another function of these structures was to keep alive the oral history of the descendants and family members. When maintenance was required, loved ones would retell the stories of the deceased; as many of the people honored with gravestones were small children, mothers, or soldiers killed in battle, the story took on a mythological dimension.

According to one theory, the inspiration behind the style in which they were built (which included adornments you might find on existing homes) was the art found in biblical texts of the late 19th century, showing the mansions in heaven.

LOIS LOFTIN DOLL MUSEUM

16

A nostalgic cruise through your personal history

204 Front Street, Deridder
337-463-5534
beauregardtourism.com
Mon–Fri 8:30am–5pm
Free admission

Inside a 1934 post office within the Beauregard Parish Tourist Office, the Lois Loftin Doll Museum is a delightful and impressive collection of dolls collected over a lifetime by Lois Loftin of Deridder. The more than 3,000 dolls that Mrs. Loftin bequeathed to Deridder now number over 4,000. About 90 percent are on display at any given time: They are occasionally rotated out so that they all get some exposure.

The variety and number are stunning and include dolls of almost every description, from antique porcelain dolls to modern icons like Raggedy Ann and an extensive collection of Barbie and Ken. As you walk past the seemingly endless glass cases, you'll probably see your fa-

vorite and maybe run across some you forgot ever existed. It can be a very nostalgic cruise through your personal history.

The 19th-century dolls were usually made from durable materials that have held up well up to the vagaries of time, whereas many of the modern dolls were designed for mass consumption and distribution. So you'd be right in saying that they don't make things like they used to … at least when it comes to dolls.

In most cases, the older dolls were made by artisans, and you can see the stunning detail in everything from the hair to the period clothing.

There are dolls of George Washington and Abraham Lincoln, Kewpie dolls from state fairs, a copy of the irreverent ventriloquist dummy Charlie McCarthy (a radio star in the 1930s and '40s), a doll that looks suspiciously like Howdy Doody, and an early TV icon that baby boomers will remember. There are also many ethnic dolls from around the world: enough to keep aficionados busy for a good hour or two.

The lifeless stares of so many of these toys might remind you of the liberal use of dolls in recent horror films, coupled with the fact that across the street is the Gothic Jail (see p. 94).

GOTHIC JAIL

17

The "Hanging Jail"

205 West 1st Street, DeRidder
337-375-3456
explorelouisiana.com/blog/gothic-deridder-jail
Daytime tours by reservation
Nighttime tours in the dark with flashlights (dubbed "Gothic Lantern") also
available on select Fridays and Saturdays. You are welcome to roam the jail
alone with your flashlight if you like
Every weekend in October and on Halloween night the jail is turned into a
haunted house

In a three-story "Collegiate Gothic"-style building in downtown De-Ridder, the Gothic Jail is a former prison that closed in 1984 and was left vacant for about 20 years. It is now a tourist destination offering daytime and nighttime tours.

Built between 1913 and 1914 by Stevens and Nelson Architects of New Orleans as a state-of-the-art jail for Beauregard Parish in western Louisiana, it became known as the "Hanging Jail," a name by which it is still known today.

The jail had cells furnished with steel bunks and housing a dozen prisoners; unusually for the time, each cell had a toilet, shower, lavatory and window. Those on the top floor also had skylights that allowed prisoners to wave to passing pedestrians from the windows.

The interior is quite spooky … naturally enough, as jails built in 1915 weren't posh accommodations! At the top of the spiral staircase, a wooden scaffold and a hanging noose are a chilling reminder of the jail's past history.

Hanged from a rope suspended from the top of the spiral staircase

The most infamous incident that led to the nickname "Hanging Jail" occurred in 1928 when J. J. Breville, a taxi driver, picked up a $1.50 fare from two men he knew, who then robbed and brutally murdered him. After a manhunt, a trial and two stays of execution, both men were hanged at the jail from a rope suspended from the top of the spiral staircase, where every inmate in the jail had a clear view of the deed. They were the only two men ever to be hanged at the jail.

There are many tales of paranormal activity at the jail: The two condemned men and the jailer are said to roam the building.

It is rumored that Disney has considered using the jail as a stand-in for buildings in films set in England, notably the Old Bailey, the Tower of London and Newgate Prison.

WAR MEMORIAL CIVIC CENTER

18

The first-ever USO

250 West 7th Street, DeRidder
337-463-7212
beauregardtourism.com/museums.html
Mon–Fri 8am–4pm

Even those with a highly developed sense of military history may not realize that it was here, in a community civic center near downtown DeRidder, that the first United Services Organization (more commonly known as a USO) was opened.

It is a type A building, the largest design used for USOs. Constructed in 39 days, it was completed eight days before the attack on Pearl Harbor and served the men and women stationed at Fort Polk and the DeRidder Army Air Base. It served as a USO until the Korean War (1950–53).

Today it appears just as it did then, with the original structure still intact and all the original plumbing, fixtures and furnishings, including the comfortable and welcoming wooden chairs.

There are cases full of war trophies such as German and Japanese uniforms and equipment, and a bazooka sitting atop the case nearest to a jukebox, surrounded by Japanese memorabilia brought back from the war.

The five meeting rooms are named for Generals Omar Bradley, Mark Clark, Dwight Eisenhower, George C. Marshall and George Patton. If you're familiar with Patton's reputation as a soldier of the old school, note that the gunnery, with its many vintage rifles and pistols, is named after him. His portrait hangs over the door.

The USO was a staple of military life during the war as a place to provide soldiers with a "home away from home" and to keep morale high. It was open to any enlisted man or woman in good standing. No drinking or fighting was allowed.

Such was the cohesiveness of a society at war that movie stars, musicians and sports heroes all showed up at the USO, some to work as waiters or even in the kitchen.

Forbidden to leave the dance with a soldier

Dances were held here three days a week: Girls were required to come alone or with their parents and to leave the same way. They were not allowed to leave with a soldier.

Today, dances are still held occasionally on the same wooden floors as in the 1940s.

Over time, there were more than 300 USOs.

"RURAL FREE DELIVERY" FRESCO ⑲

A skilful portrayal of rural life in the 1930s

204 Fron Street, DeRidder
337-463-5534
beauregardtourism.com
Mon–Fri 8:30am–5pm

A colorful fresco depicting a rural mail delivery adorns the walls of the Beauregard Tourist Commission Office in DeRidder, now in the old post office. The work is by renowned artist Conrad Albrizio, an art instructor at LSU.

Twenty-three murals and other artworks under the auspices of the WPA (Works Progress Administration) were funded in Louisiana post offices. The only fresco is this one.

The U.S. federal government recognized the need to reach out to artists and writers who were all hurt by the scarcity of work in the 1930s after the Wall Street Crash of 1929. At the time, professional artists were paid $38.20 a week, and laborers (who often built ornamental bridges, benches, parks and other recreational facilities) $13.70 a week.

Albrizio, who was paid $550 for the mural, was required to submit sketches before being awarded the contract. He asked for input from the community and, as DeRidder's economy was fueled by lumber and farming, he chose to have a herdsman and a farmer in his composition.

The committee awarding the contract had a couple of suggestions. They did not care for Albrizio's first idea of having a mailman on a motorcycle, even though this was a common sight in those days.

At first, the artist had two men in the composition but then changed it to show a farmer in a field, sitting on a rail and reading his mail while tending to the sheep. He replaced the motorcycle-riding mailman with a mail deliverer on horseback to satisfy the community's wish to portray the rural life they were familiar with.

Upon examining the post office walls, Albrizio decided that the surface was a suitable base for a fresco. Finding that he needed a thicker, more stable plaster base, he hired a professional plasterer to smooth and prepare the surface for his final coat, as the painting of the fresco would often leave his hands trembling from the physical exertion involved. This added significantly to his expenses as he was also required to pay for all materials and their transport himself.

Albrizio started the work in July of 1936 and finished in the fall, working between semesters at LSU, where he was head of the Art Department.

The fresco is a fine example of 1930s art deco "Depression" style and is very similar to the murals at Allen Hall in LSU, where Albrizio's students painted scenes of Louisiana life in the 1930s.

Acadiana

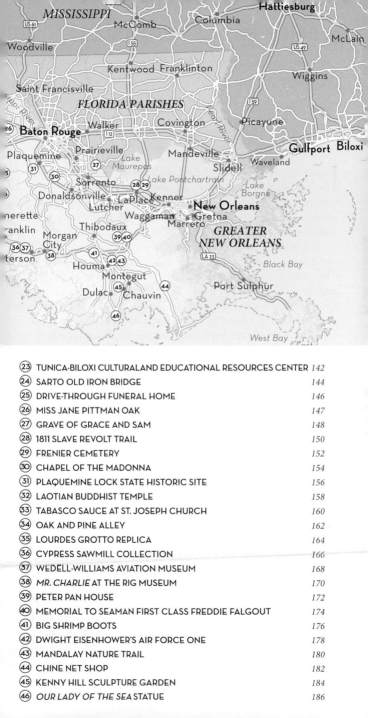

MISSISSIPPI
US 61 McComb Columbia Hattiesburg
Woodville US 49 McLain
I 55
Kentwood Franklinton
Saint Francisville Wiggins
FLORIDA PARISHES I 59
Baton Rouge Walker Covington Picayune
I 12
Plaquemine Prairieville Mandeville Gulfport Biloxi
Lake Maurepas Slidell Waveland
31 30 Sorrento 28 29 Lake Pontchartrain Lake Borgne
Donaldsonville LaPlace Kenner
Lutcher Waggaman New Orleans
nerette Thibodaux Marrero Gretna
anklin Morgan 39 40 GREATER NEW ORLEANS
36 37 City 41 LA 23
terson 38 Houma 42 43 Black Bay
Montegut
Dulac 45 Chauvin 44 Port Sulphur
46 West Bay

A BRICK BAS-RELIEF MURAL

Techniques that go back to the time of Nebuchadnezzar II

Sulphur Regional Library
1160 Cypress Street, Sulphur
337-721-7138 – calcasieulibaray.org/sulphur-library
Mon–Thurs 9am–8pm, Fri 9am–6pm, Sat 9am–5pm, Sun 1pm–5pm

Inside Sulphur Regional Library, the *History of the City of Sulphur* by artist Paula Collins is a stunning 6-ft. x 16-ft. brick bas-relief mural that depicts sulfur mines, shrimp boats, cowboys, oil exploration, flora, animals (pelicans, alligators, deer, ducks) as well as farming and cattle and other industries from the history of West Calcasieu Parish.

The work is a carved image in 3D. Its ancient architectural technique and brownish hue are reminiscent of Chaldean or Assyrian bas reliefs. The warmth created by the method results in a finished product that goes beyond a normal flat mural. The technique, which goes back to the time of Nebuchadnezzar II, requires the unfired brick, while still malleable, to be wrapped in a material so that it remains moist and workable. The bricks are stacked on a plywood easel and the sketch or picture to be portrayed is drawn onto the "green" bricks. Then the carving of the figures starts, using a variety of shaping tools, including linoleum knives, wood-carving tools and general construction tools. The bricks are the consistency of well-frozen ice cream and are sprayed with water to maintain a moist enough texture to remain workable. The texture is then applied by scraping, tapping, or rolling the surface with various objects.

When the carving is finished, the bricks are disassembled, and each brick is numbered so that the full picture can be recreated faithfully. The bricks are then dried and fired in a kiln before being installed at the mural's location. Once at the installation site, the artist supervises the bricklayers. After the artist has done the final touch-ups to ensure the continuity of the image and scraped off any mortar, the bricks are sprayed with an anti-graffiti seal to prevent vandalism.

CHARPENTIER HISTORIC DISTRICT

Discovering new gems around each corner

Get off at Interstate 10 Exit 31A, Lake Charles
Roughly 40 square blocks bounded by Interstate 10 on the North, Boston Street
on the East, Kirby to the South, and Ryan to the East
337-491-1429; 337-436-9588
Info on tours: Lake Charles Southwest Convention and Visitors Center
Free app from Lake Charles Historic Tourist Bureau

Even many architects are unaware of the Charpentier Historic District, a whole area in Lake Charles that is home to a distinctive Louisiana architectural style: This 40-block, 158-acre neighborhood just off I-10 on the north shore of Lake Charles, next to the historic downtown, is a showcase of Victorian do-it-yourself architecture.

The homes built here from the 1880s up until 1939 were a result of the timber boom in the late 1800s. At that time, there were no practicing architects in Lake Charles, so each house resulted from the personal vision and talent of the carpenters who built them, each trying to outdo the other with architectural flourishes of curlicue woodwork, balconies, porches, distinctive columns and pillars, and steeped roofs.

What resulted is an enduring urban neighborhood filled with houses of various Victorian styles, a combination of styles and designs that led the Louisiana state architectural historian Jonathan Fricker to coin the term "Lake Charles-style architecture."

Although you can easily drive yourself and discover new gems around each corner, you can also arrange a tour of some of the buildings at the Lake Charles Southwest Convention and Visitors Center.

W. H. TUPPER STORE MUSEUM

A trip back in time

311 North Main Street, Jennings
337-821-5532
tuppermuseum@cityofjennings.com
Mon–Fri 9am–5pm

The W. H. Tupper Store Museum offers an authentic trip back in time: The former store and its contents are not replicas, they are the contents just as they were in 1949 when the store was closed.

A successful farmer (among other things), W. H. Tupper opened his General Merchandise store in 1910 just north of Jennings, near Elton. It was originally just for his employees. You could find pretty much everything you needed at the store, so Mr. Tupper eventually opened it to the general public.

After his death, the remaining family members could not agree on the course forward for the store, so in 1949 they closed it, packed up all the contents, and put them into storage. At some point, it was decided to move the store and its contents to Jennings and create a museum.

You'll find name brands like Kleenex (a box sold for 17 cents), Log Cabin syrup (31 cents), and Wrigley's gum. These products are 'as is,'

still in their boxes and packs, and are found just as they were in 1949.

There are also musical instruments like a Hohner accordion, just waiting for an Acadian child to bring it to life, and a Hohner harmonica still in its box.

An interesting product that you're not likely to see in a regular store anytime soon, such as fireworks, hints at how times have changed. (Fireworks are now against the law in most metropolitan areas of the U.S.). Firecrackers, Roman candles, sparklers, and repeating bombs still lie in their packages next to other products.

There are clothes for the entire family: menswear, women's fashions, and even children's and baby things, including a nice supply of Johnson & Johnson baby powder. The hats – both men's and women's – are right out of a period piece movie.

Apparently, the most valuable pieces of merchandise are the vintage toys and games. As old toys are highly collectible, it's hard to say what their worth would be today.

All in all, the museum gives a fascinating glimpse into yesteryear.

And if this is not enough nostalgia for you, go into the adjoining room: Here you'll find the Telephone Pioneer Museum, with vintage telephones going back over 100 years as well as hundreds of other tools, parts and phone memorabilia.

LA MAISON DE BEGNAUD

A deep dive into the area's unique culture

110 Benoit Patin Road, Scott
337-269-5155
mamaredell@yahoo.com
Bourrée game every other Wed

Right off of Interstate 10 in Scott, La Maison de Begnaud is a wooden Cajun cottage that hosts a Bourrée game every other Wednesday. At these biweekly sessions, the public is invited to play and learn this card game, which is a touchstone of Cajun culture.

The game has its regulars and Bourrée is renowned for its potentially cutthroat nature: Players can lose large sums of money depending on the stakes and how the cards fall. At the Begnaud Center, the game takes on a much friendlier tone that displays the incredibly hospitable and social nature of Cajun culture.

Each player gets a bag of poker chips, and the game is on. Bourrée is thought to be derived from a three-card game in southwest France with roots going back to a Spanish card game named Burru, which means donkey in Spanish. The donkey here is presumably the player who goes "Bourrée" and has to match the pot. Simply, it can be described as a form of five-card bridge.

The purpose of the game, which is played with a standard 52-card deck, is to acquire the most tricks. The game is played by from two to eight players, seven being the optimal number.

A simple explanation of the game is that each player is dealt five cards face down and the dealer throws his last card face up to establish the trump suit. Players then proceed in a clockwise direction to either pass or play. Those who pass are eliminated from winning the pot.

At the end of the game, if any player fails to win a trump, they are said to have "Bourréed" and they must match the pot which carries over to the next dealt hand. This means that, in a serious game of Bourrée, the pot may grow quite large and the stakes may be high.

If no one wins the pot (as there may be a tie for trumps won), the pot carries over to the next hand. This is another feature of the game that lends itself to large pots won and lost. Many games have a limit on how much must be put into the pot ... which does restrict the chances of losing your shirt.

Here at Begnaud's the game is played for the fun, camaraderie and educational value of sharing a cultural experience. If you Bourrée in this game, you only have to ante up two chips as the penalty.

The quaint cottage also showcases other important Cajun institutional traditions, including regular music jams.

Boureki (a very similar game to Bourrée) is played on the Greek island of Psara.

THE TREES OF SOLES

Hang your burdens and make them lighter

Take Exit 97 on I-10 at Scott
Drive north on Louisiana Highway 93 for 2.5 miles
Take a left at Cocodril Road for 2 miles

On a dusty gravel country road about 2 miles from Louisiana Highway 93, it may take time and perseverance to find three tall trees decorated in a haphazard way with numerous pairs of shoes twined by shoelaces, nailed to the trees, or attached any which way the owner of the shoes could think of.

These are the Trees of Soles, a play on words (soles and souls), which provide a sense of pedestrian wonder for the visitor who stumbles upon them as they sit in a rather off-the-beaten-path spot.

Humanity has a way of finding endless ways to connect to the spiritual universe and few are as creative and touching as the Trees of Soles. A sign explains that the trees are places to hang your burdens and make them lighter.

You can bring footwear that may have been worn in difficult times of your life and throw it up into the limbs of the trees or nail it to the trunks if you desire. There are no cut-and-dried rituals although the long wind-up and toss toward the sky seems to be the preferred method.

And shoes do end up here. A lot of them. Tennis shoes, sandals, clogs, cowboy boots, dress shoes, rubber wading boots, flip flops, Nikes, baby shoes and women's pumps to name a few.

The trees have inspired and touched many who come to see them. The message is clearly a Christian one with references to Jesus central to the sign, but the inspirational message conjured from simple everyday things has a decidedly uplifting tone here.

Originally there was just one Tree of Soles. It was knocked down by Hurricane Lili in 2002.

An added plus (especially for those who are new to the area) is the fact that Exit 97 is kind of a Cajun specialty meat mecca. There are at least four large Cajun meat markets and for those who wish to partake of this south Louisiana treat, that is reason enough to stop at Scott.

"Frog Capital of the World"

Throughout the town of Rayne

"Father Joe"
St. Joseph Church

U pon entering the small Cajun prairie town of Rayne from Interstate 10, you'll be greeted by a galvanized aluminum frog statue wearing a top hat and tails. This is just the beginning of your frog immersion as you'll almost immediately see concrete frogs all over town. Each statue is painted to suit its location or the sponsor who maintains it.

You'll also see numerous murals dedicated to Rayne's association with the frog, and indeed Rayne bills itself as the 'Frog Capital of the World'.

Rayne has another claim to fame as the official Louisiana City of Murals, a title it attained in the 1990s after a beautification board commissioned world-renowned muralist Robert Dafford to paint a series of large murals on downtown buildings. Other businesses have followed suit and now Rayne boasts 30 murals, most of which celebrate the frog in one way or another.

A Frog Festival

The story started when a gourmet chef named Donat Pucheu decided to export frog legs to popular restaurants in New Orleans in the 1880s. Then Jacques Weil and his brothers traveled from France to Rayne and were so taken with the local frogs that they decided to market them to the world. At one time in its heyday, the Weil brothers were exporting 10,000 lb. of frog legs a week.

Sardi's, a famous New York eatery, had them prominently on their menu, billing Rayne as the Frog Capital of the World.

Today the frog industry has wound down and, in an attempt to keep the frog brand alive, Rayne started a Frog Festival in 1973 that is still going strong. Since 2015, the Rayne Frog Festival has been held every Mother's Day weekend.

Frogging remains a large part of the local fabric and it is not uncommon to find couples stalking the local frog population on a date night. A date night of frogging means competing with snakes for the delicacy.

J.D. MILLER RECORDING STUDIO MUSEUM ⑦

All due to the musical entrepreneurship of J.D. Miller

Crowley City Hall
425 North Parkerson Avenue, Crowley
337-783-0824
crowley-la.com/tourism
Mon–Thurs 8am– 4:30pm, Fri 8am–noon

Inside a former Ford dealership in the center of old Crowley, you'll find not one but two small museums: one dedicated to the overwhelming importance of rice to Acadiana and particularly Crowley (first floor), the other to a native son, J.D. Miller, a pioneer in swamp pop and other genres.

On the second floor, at the J.D. Miller Recording Studio Museum, you'll discover that many of the hits that make up the mosaic of the American songbook emanated from every corner of the United States ... and none more so than here in Crowley from the musical entrepreneurship and pen of J.D. Miller.

The small museum displays the numerous record labels that Miller created and recorded under. It also has a map of the southern United States that highlights some of the more prominent smaller studios that ranged from Georgia across Tennessee down to Alabama, Louisiana, and as far west as Houston. These were essential breeding grounds for rock'n'roll, country, blues, swamp pop, swamp blues, zydeco and Cajun music to bring the sounds of the rich and diverse musical motherlode that was American pop in the 20th century.

Some of the equipment Miller used – the music machines and recorders of the 1950 and 1960s – are displayed here, with Miller represented by a mannequin in a pose operating his machines.

Miller's parents bought him an $8 guitar and a Gene Autry songbook from the Sears catalog when he was 11. Aged 13, he won a contest and secured a regular gig that paid him $5 a week for a 15-minute radio show. In the 1950s, he recorded swamp pop records, which had a significant influence on the popular music of America.

In 1952 Miller wrote the song "It Wasn't God Who Made Honky Tonk Angels." Kitty Wells and Webb Pierce both had hits with this single. Wells's version was Number One on the country charts for six weeks and sold over a million copies – the first woman to have a Number One country hit. This gave Miller a lot of cachet with the Nashville record producers.

Miller's reputation and the quality of his music would lure more mainstream artists to his Crowley studio. Paul Simon recorded "That Was Your Mother" on his Graceland album in Miller's studio.

As a songwriter, Miller penned notable hits, such as "I Hear You Knockin," covered by The Fabulous Thunderbirds, Dwight Yoakam and Tom Jones. He wrote "Diggy Liggy Lo", which was a hit for Cajun legend Doug Kershaw. Slim Harpo's "Rainin' in My Heart", recorded on a Miller label, was covered by both the Rolling Stones and Neil Young. The Kinks covered "I'm a Lover, Not a Fighter."

GRAND OPERA HOUSE OF THE SOUTH

A large dose of elegant nostalgia

505 North Parkerson Avenue, Crowley
337-785-0440
thegrandoperahouse.org
Mon–Fri 8am–noon

In a revitalized downtown Crowley, the rice capital of Louisiana, a once almost forgotten masterpiece sits inside a four-story building. After entering a marquee that says "Grand", you see an exquisite wooden staircase that rises to the second floor and then you anticipate what awaits inside.

The sight is breathtaking as you enter a fully remodeled and restored theater that brings you back to the early 20th century. It looks just like

the theaters you see in period films before silent or talking movies when America's entertainers toiled and dazzled in the footlights.

The building was constructed in 1901 by a livery stable owner/sheriff and for nearly 40 years it served as hub of activity in Crowley, bringing national and international stars to Acadiana. Among the luminaries who graced its stage were Enrico Caruso, Clark Gable, Huey Long, Madame de Vilchez-Bisset of the Paris Opera, and even Babe Ruth.

The award-winning design that brought the theater back to life was the brainchild of architect Donald J. Breaux. It features four boxes close to the stage with plush armchairs upholstered in gold fabric, and angel medallions hand-painted by local artist Rhonda Stevens. The overall look of the mostly wooden structure is retro, with a large dose of elegant nostalgia. The building measures 33,000 sq. feet and seats 400.

The first floor had as colorful a history as the theater, as it once housed a saloon, a cafe, a mortuary and a pool hall. It was an early 20th-century mini-mall with vaudeville shows upstairs and later it also showed silent and talking films.

On the second floor, you'll find a small museum that testifies to the rich history of this building, with period clothing and theatrical costumes, props, photos and original playbills.

Closed around 1940, the building sat silent yet mostly intact, said to be all but forgotten as downtown Crowley (like so many once thriving small town main streets) fell on hard times. The renovation of the space and its resurrection are credited with revitalizing the downtown area of Crowley.

In 1999, philanthropist and entrepreneur L. J. Gielen purchased the building and started on the task of restoring it. In 2004, it was turned over by the Gielen family to a non-profit that runs it today. Since 2008, with the help of funds from the state of Louisiana and the federal government as well as local organizations, it has been back in business with a vengeance. National, international and local talent grace the stage regularly.

It is now truly a community space. Local children and teenagers can and do get their start on the same stage where the most famous acts in showbiz appeared. The local kids often leave a mark backstage as their contribution to the arts scene.

The Grand Opera House of the South prospered back in the day because of the presence of the railroad, the track being only a few blocks away from the theater. As Crowley was halfway between New Orleans and Houston, it was also a natural spot for travelers and entertainers to stop for the night.

STEEN'S SYRUP CANS

Each storage silo holds 16,683 gallons of pure cane syrup

119 North Main Street, Abbeville
800-725-1654
steenssyrup.com

On North Main Street in Abbeville, three sizeable yellow syrup storage cans are painted to look like the iconic syrup cans that the people of Louisiana (and indeed the southern United States) have used for years to sweeten their lives.

Replicas of the product container that has been on the shelves of stores since 1910, the large cans indicate that each storage silo holds 16,683 gallons of pure cane syrup. They also boast of the purity of the product: 'NOTHING ADDED. NOTHING EXTRACTED.'

The cans are, of course, local landmarks and a subject of pride to locals, who appreciate the national and even international recognition of an enterprise born and bred in Abbeville on the banks of the Vermilion River.

Sugar has been a symbol (and the economic powerhouse) of Louisiana since Jesuits brought the cane plants to the area well over 200 years ago.

In 1910, an early freeze threatened sugar growers like Charlie Steen with substantial financial losses. However, Steen was quite the go-getter and an innovator. He had initially been a successful blacksmith in the Abbeville area – so successful that he opened a sawmill, a corn mill and a cotton gin. Sugar was a side hustle.

Faced with the total loss of his 600-ton crop of sugar cane, Steen improvised. He built a small mule-driven mill, the first of its kind in the world, to grind his cane crop and extract the juice, and he simmered the product in large open kettles to create the pure cane syrup that has become famous throughout the kitchens of the south.

Steen family lore does admit that this first batch produced three barrels of putrid, thick, sour syrup. But Charlie was encouraged and learned from his mistakes and soon other farmers were bringing their crops to him for processing.

The company is now in its fourth generation and still uses the original recipes, process and equipment to create its syrup.

The yellow cans have become famous over the century and changed not at all. Steen's 100% Pure Cane Syrup has become such a well-known brand that you can find recipes specifying it by name in the archives of almost every major newspaper and magazine in the U.S.

The sweet, thick, pure syrup is a throwback to a more calorie-rich diet. Still, its continued existence is a comforting fact for many Louisianans, whose famous regional cuisine is a point of great local pride.

From October into December, the sweet process's aroma permeates the air of Abbeville.

THE HISTORY OF MEDICINE IN LOUISIANA MURAL

Almost lost to history

Edith Garland Dupré Library,
Lafayette
600 East St. Mary Boulevard
337-482-6025
louisiana.edu/directory/dupre-library

About 100 ft. to your right, overlooking the Reference & Research Services area as you enter the Edith Garland Dupré Library at the University of Louisiana in Lafayette, *The History of Medicine in Louisiana* mural has been called 'probably the most unique piece of artwork in Louisiana,' although it was almost lost to history.

The 112-ft. x 57-in. semi-abstract mural is a survey of different milestones in the medical history of the State of Louisiana. It represents the steady progress from Native American medicine men's use of sucking tubes, charms and magic to treat the sick, to the atomic age and the use of isotope tracers in the bloodstream.

Across the mural from left to right, we see: de Bienville draining the

swamp around New Orleans as a public health move, Francois Marie Precost performing the first Caesarean section in the United States, the 1853 yellow fever epidemic that claimed 12,000 lives in Louisiana and other significant events that led to better healthcare in Louisiana.

The mural was commissioned in 1960 by the Aloe Company, a medical supply company based in New Orleans. For two years, the artist Franklin Boggs worked exclusively on the project in Wisconsin at Beloit College although he traveled to New Orleans many times to research the subject.

After 25 years on display at the Aloe Company, the artwork was moved to Tulane Medical Center in New Orleans and then went into storage, where it was all but forgotten. Fifteen years later, a group of people who knew of the mural's existence tried to save it. Dr. and Mrs. Thomas F. Kraemer of Franklin were instrumental in getting the work moved to the University of Louisiana at Lafayette. The panels were restored by noted muralists Robert Dafford and Wayne Ditch, with financial support from the Teche Federal Savings Bank, the Friends of the Edith Garland Dupré Library and the University of Louisiana at Lafayette Foundation.

The stunning mural was finally installed on the first floor of the library in 2002.

BRONZE STATUE OF ROSA PARKS

Sit next to Rosa Parks

Rosa Parks Transportation Center
100 Lee Avenue, Lafayette
Mon–Fri 8am–5pm

In the heart of Lafayette, a life-size bronze statue of Rosa Parks lies appropriately enough in the Transportation Center station lobby. Sitting on a bus seat looking out of the window in the iconic pose captured from a UPI photograph, the statue with Parks gazing to her left supplies a beau-

tiful photo op as the seat next to her is empty and just the right size for someone to sit next to the civil rights icon.

On December 1, 1955, Rosa Parks, a seamstress at a local Montgomery, Alabama, department store, refused the bus driver's order to move toward the back of the bus to accommodate a white rider as was the law at that time in Alabama.

Her action inspired the National Association for the Advancement of Colored People (NAACP) to organize the celebrated bus boycott of the Montgomery transit system, which lasted for over a year and was a highlight of the struggle for equality by African Americans in the United States.

By her actions and the subsequent ruling by the U.S. federal courts in the case Browder v. Gayle, Parks established that the Alabama law which segregated the bus system was a violation of the 14th Amendment, which provides equal protection under the law for all citizens.

She was honored by an act of Congress as "the first lady of civil rights" and "the mother of the freedom movement."

There are numerous statues honoring Rosa Parks in the United States and around the world, including a statue in the National Statuary Hall at the U.S. Capitol building.

VICE PRESIDENTIAL LIVE OAK

12

One of the most majestic live oaks in the world

914 St. John Street, Lafayette
Next to the Cathedral of St. John the Evangelist
lgcfinc.org/live-oak-society.html

I n the grounds of the Cathedral of St. John the Evangelist, in the middle of downtown Lafayette, the St. John Oak is one of the most majestic live oaks in the world. Estimated to be over 450 years old, it measured 19 ft. in circumference in 1929 and had grown to 29 ft. 6 in. by 2015.

Today, the tree is surrounded by fencing to protect its extensive root system, and some of its ancient spreading limbs have been reinforced with strategically placed poles.

Many people believe that the reason the cathedral was built here in the first place was because of the presence of this magnificent live oak.

The Live Oak Society: Each tree has its own attorney

The live oak is one of the defining images of Acadiana, and it should be no surprise that the Live Oak Society was born here in Lafayette. Inspired by the abundance and beauty of the live oaks, Dr. Edwin Lewis Stephens, the first president of Southwestern Louisiana Institute (now the University of Louisiana at Lafayette, or ULL), founded the society in 1934 with the aim of promoting the culture, distribution and appreciation of the live oak. Today, the society boasts as members over 10,000 trees found across 15 states. To qualify as a member, a live oak must be at least 100 years old. The society has its own rules: Each tree has an "attorney", or sponsor; and once upon a time, each tree was required to pay dues of 25 acorns a year. Trees can be expelled for bearing advertising or for being whitewashed. Only one human is a member of the society: the honorary chairman. The current president of the Live Oak Society is the Seven Sisters Oak in Mandeville, Louisiana. The St. John Cathedral Oak is the second vice president.

MISS ROSE'S BAR: HAPPY MAN SCULPTURE

Created for the 1984 World's Fair

1400 Northwest Evangeline Thruway, Lafayette
Take exit 103A off Interstate 10
Drive south on 167/Evangeline Parkway

At the Lafayette welcome center parking lot on Acadian Thruway, right after you get off Interstate 10 at exit 103A and drive towards downtown, two silvery cartoonish figures depicting a barmaid and a bar customer sit under a canopy of trees.

The trees almost hide the sculpture from the street. You have to drive off the thruway and into the welcome center before seeing something … but it might not come into focus till you get pretty close. This means that you could pass it by your whole life and not notice it.

The *Miss Rose's Bar: Happy Man* sculpture is said to depict Miss Rose, the proprietress of a neighborhood bar, together with a bar patron, and underlines the importance of such institutions in African American culture.

Exhibited at the 1984 World's Fair in New Orleans, the sculpture was created by Albert LaVergne, Professor Emeritus at Western Michigan University. LaVergne grew up in rural Louisiana, the son of a sharecropper, and credits his father's insistence that all his children had to acquire skills as the path to him becoming an artist. Working with farm tools, having to fix equipment and invent tools, observing machinery working in town,

and digging red clay out of the farmland to create animal statues all prepared LaVergne for his later work as a renowned sculptor.

After the fair, the sculpture changed hands more than once and ended up abandoned and left to decay and rust in a pasture in Acadiana. When it was discovered wasting away, the Rotary Club North of Lafayette volunteered money and labor to restore it and move it to its present location.

LaVergne's work is now found all over the world, with some notable pieces in Nigeria.

NEARBY
Roman crane: a technology used well into the 19th century (14)

Outside of Fletcher Hall, University of Louisiana, Lafayette
337-482-1000

Tucked behind Fletcher Hall on the campus of the University of Louisiana at Lafayette, an impressive wooden wheel usually puzzles visitors to this part of the campus. Featured in a 2010 Discovery episode of the TV show Engineering the Impossible, this life-size model of a Roman crane was designed by Dr. Chris Carroll, an engineering professor at ULL, and his students. The Romans were true masters at building these cranes: The Pentaspastos crane utilized 5 pulleys and could move even more, whereas the Polyspaston crane, with 15 pulleys and 4 masts, could move weights at a 50:1 ratio and would allow for the movement of 12,000 pounds. Roman crane technology was used well into the 19th century to build some of the largest monuments in Europe. Dr. Carroll and his team were called upon again in 2013 to replicate Egyptian architectural engineering in a Science Channel show entitled Unearthing Ancient Secrets.

NATIVE AMERICAN STATUE

A sculpture so large that it's taller than the roof of the home

607 Gerald Drive, Lafayette
Private residence

Between two tall trees on the front lawn of a suburban home in Lafayette, a huge 13-ft. sculpture of a Native American may come as a surprise for many. As lawn ornaments go, this well-formed warrior, with an ax in one hand and a knife in the other, is not only unique but BIG! Weighing over 2,000 lb., it's so large that it's taller than the roof of the home. Even If you know it's there, it still impresses with its size.

In 2004, Charlie Deville found himself at an auction in New Jersey. Being one-eighth Chitimacha (a local Native American tribe in southern Louisiana) and related to two chiefs of the Chitimacha through his great grandmother, he was taken with the statue.

Deville purchased it for $13,500 (without freight) and then had it shipped to his plantation, Lawtell, back in Louisiana. In 2016, he moved to more modest digs in a subdivision in Lafayette and had the statue planted on his front lawn. It is anchored by a spike that keeps it stable during the periodic hurricanes.

According to press reports and an online description of the unusual lawn art, his neighbors seem to like the 13-ft. statue.

Charlie is an avid collector of Native American artifacts. He has a 500-lb. bronze Comanche statue in his bedroom, and wants his ashes placed inside it when he passes away. He says it was an easy move to bring the huge statue from its old to its new home. It only took him 15 minutes to set it up in the yard.

Charlie is more than alright with passersby coming for a look and doesn't mind if you stand in the yard to admire the statue and take photos. He says it's there to be enjoyed.

MARTIN ACCORDIONS WORKSHOP

16

Some of the most beautifully crafted musical instruments you'll ever see, in a hard-to-find spot

2143 West Willow Street, Lafayette
337-232-4001
martinaccordions.com
Mon–Fri 8am–5pm, Sat 8am–noon

If you didn't know better, you'd think the two dilapidated old wooden buildings at 2143 West Willow Street were permanently shuttered. You'd never guess that one of them holds a workshop where some of the most beautifully crafted musical instruments you'll ever see are made – instruments that are integral to Acadiana music and culture. The buildings bear no noticeable signage; however, if you poke around a little, you'll soon find the entrance to an almost hidden music workshop.

Step through the door, and you'll find yourself standing in the Martin Accordions workshop, where some of the meticulously hand-crafted instruments are built. To the right, lined up along their cases, are gleaming authentic Acadian accordions bearing the Martin's signature crawfish logo.

To your left, you're likely to encounter a craftsman fashioning his next musical work of art. You may even meet Clarence "Junior" Martin, one of the fewer than 30 master accordion makers left in Louisiana, who keep this decidedly Cajun craft alive.

Visitors are encouraged to drop in to observe these musical artisans at work. Folks are friendly here, and they don't mind if guests ask questions or start up a conversation. Of course, you should remember that this is a serious workspace where the accordion-makers must concentrate on their craft.

Martin's, "Cajun Accordions" are of such high quality that they are today well known throughout the world, even in Germany, where the instrument was first patented in 1822.

The history of this unique instrument is a classic American tale, as German, French, and African American musicians all seem to have had a significant hand in its evolution and, consequently, its music. Note that Jewish merchants imported the accordion to the small towns of Acadiana. Late-19th-century catalogs, such as those of Sears Roebuck and Montgomery Ward, also allowed widespread access to the instruments.

The popularity of the accordion waxed and waned in the first part of the 20th century, becoming popular again in the 1940s. However, the advent of World War II eliminated the German accordion, as the factories there were destroyed. This led Cajun accordion lovers in Louisiana to hone their skills at making new instruments after learning how to repair accordions from materials salvaged from the older instruments.

SHRINE OF ST. JOHN BERCHMANS ⑰

America's only shrine at the exact location of a Vatican-confirmed miracle

1821 Academy Rd, Grand Coteau
337-662-5275
rscj.org/miracle-grand-coteau
By appointment only

In Grand Coteau, the Shrine of St. John Berchmans is the only shrine at the exact location of a Vatican-confirmed miracle in the United States. A former infirmary, this small simple chapel with an altar and a few pews was turned into a shrine after the miracle by St. John Berchmans, whose intercession on behalf of a novice nun called Mary Wilson resulted in her miraculous recovery.

Born in 1846 in Canada, Mary Wilson moved to Louisiana in 1866: It was thought that the gentler climate of south Louisiana would be beneficial for her poor health. But she became dangerously ill, vomiting blood two or three times a day, with constant fever and violent headaches. She had not eaten an ounce of food for about 40 days when, according to Mary's handwritten account, she put a holy card of John

S. GIOVANNI BERCHMANS S. I.

Berchmans on her mouth and asked, "If it be true that you can work miracles, I wish you would do something for me." At that point, Mary says she heard a whisper: "Open your mouth." She said it felt like someone had put a finger on her tongue and it gave her immediate relief from the pain. The voice continued to tell her, "Sister, you will get the desired habit. Be faithful. Have confidence. Fear not." Mary recovered fully.

On his arrival the next day, the doctor almost fainted. The sister on duty at the time said that the doctor needed more attention than the patient!

The holy card of St. John Berchmans that Mary pressed to her lips is on display at the shrine.

Mary Wilson is buried in the nearby cemetery with the word *miraculee* on her gravestone.

Under the auspices of the Society of the Sacred Heart at Grand Coteau, the school is the oldest institution of learning in the United States, west of the Mississippi. St. Philippine Duchesne was instrumental in establishing the convent in 1821. During the Civil War, Grand Coteau became the headquarters of General Nathaniel Banks of the Union Army. As General Banks' daughter attended a Sacred Heart school in New York, he was asked by the superiors there to protect the students and nuns at the Sacred Heart in Grand Coteau. He provided food and other necessities and allowed the school to remain open during the war.

ORPHAN TRAIN MUSEUM

A poignant story

223 South Academy Street, Opelousas
337-948-9922
laorphantrainmuseum.com
Tue–Fri 10am–3pm, Sat by appointment
Admission charge

I n the heart of Opelousas, at the Le Vieux Village Complex, the Orphan Train Museum recalls a poignant story: Many of the orphans
who grew into adulthood did not even know about the train as it was
not talked about freely at the time.

In the early 1900s, there was a large orphan population in places like New York City. At a time when social services (where they even existed) were in their infancy in America, the New York Foundling Hospital was run by the Sisters of Charity. The sisters reached out to the wider Catholic communities around the United States with an appeal to take these children in.

The people of Opelousas responded in a big way. In 1907, the first orphan train arrived in the town. One man, Rev. John Engberink, a priest in Opelousas, had gone to New York to claim the children with orders from the Catholic communities of Opelousas. Parents there would get a receipt telling them when their children would arrive. Each child had a number, and the parents would have a matching number.

Opelousas at that time was a mostly French-speaking community, which apparently proved confusing for the new arrivals. Siblings were sometimes separated because of the language differences. In at least one case, a brother and sister were separated at the station and were only reunited 60 years later.

The Sisters of Charity and the church took assiduous notes of the children's passage and arrival to keep track of them and to make sure they were not abused and had been placed in loving environments.

Today, there are hundreds of descendants of the orphans who arrived from New York in 1907 and 1920. The museum was started by some of these descendants, and there is a brick memorial with the names of family members who were on those trains or are descended from them.

The museum has large numbers of photos, train benches, train station carts, and numerous examples of the clothes that the orphans were wearing when they arrived. There is also a mural by artist Robert Dafford depicting the train's arrival in 1907. It shows an orderly scene with Father Engberink in a prominent position. However, oral history contends that the situation was rather more chaotic than the mural might indicate!

In 2020, Alice Kearns Bernar remembered her arrival: "I had a tag in the bottom of my little dress. I was addressed to the people because they had ordered me through the Catholic priest to come there. I was sent like a package." Her dress and tag can be seen in the museum.

Today, the Sisters of Charity in New York help descendants of the orphan train trace their lineage.

The Orphan Train Museum in Opelousas is one of two such museums in the United States. The other is in Concordia, Kansas.

CAJUN FRENCH MUSIC HALL OF FAME

The music at the heart of this distinctive American culture

240 South C C Duson Street, Eunice
337-457-6534
cajuntravel.com/things/cajun-french-music-hall-of-fame-museum/]
Winter: Wed–Sat 8:30am–4:30pm
Summer: 9am–5pm

In the heart of Eunice, amid the Cajun Prairie, the Cajun French Music Hall of Fame is an Acadian cottage that could have been a former hardware or feed store. Blending in with its surroundings, the attraction has a surprisingly homey feel and gives a heartfelt survey of the music at the heart of this distinctive American culture. It is dedicated to those who pioneered, developed and promoted the evolution of Cajun music.

Along the walls are photos and descriptions of the greats of Cajun music, numerous artifacts and memorabilia in glass cases, and several

vintage Victrolas with old records sitting as if ready to be played. An explanatory text recalls the importance of the accordion, the instrument at the heart of modern Cajun music.

In one corner is an exhibit depicting three musicians: one with an accordion, one with a fiddle and still another with a triangle, the other key instrument of Cajun music. Although these three instruments were the original trinity of this music, others have been incorporated as the genre reached a wider audience after the appearance of Cajun musicians at the 1964 Newport Folk Festival. The washboard is also now a staple of the genre.

Cajun music played in space

One notable exhibit is a display dedicated to the Space Shuttle Atlantis which, from November 12 to November 20, 1985, brought a CD to the space station Mir and played Cajun music for the whole world to hear. The certificate, together with the CD, was signed by the Atlantis STS-74 astronauts, including the commander, Kenneth Cameron.

LE TOURNOI DE LA VILLE PLATTE

An idea straight out of the Knights of the Round Table

North Side Civic Center, Ville Platte
704 North Soileau Street
337-224-8985
evangelineparishtourism.org/le-louisiana-tournoi-de-ville-platt

Every October, a horseback jousting competition with medieval European roots, with riders dressed as knights and their steeds also in faux armor, takes place in Ville Platte. Le Tournoi de la Ville Platte is a one-of-a-kind event organized in conjunction with the Cotton Festival – in recent years, it has become the traditional ending of the festival.

The 20 riders compete in three heats as they race their equine chargers around a quarter-mile track at breakneck speed – the idea is right out of the Knights of the Round Table. On a 5-ft. wooden lance, the riders try to capture seven rings (each 2.5 in. in diameter) suspended from poles around the track. A perfect score for the three rounds would be 21 rings while covering the track in less than 14 seconds in each round. It takes great skill, horsemanship and concentration.

Some may remember a governor's race in Louisiana in the 1980s, when one of the candidates made a TV commercial in which he rode a horse and tried to spear the rings. Those from Ville Platte knew what he was doing, but most of the voters in Louisiana watching it were somewhat mystified as this is a very local event.

The riders' apparel – usually silver fabric tunics – is more akin to a Mardi Gras costume than the actual chain mail as worn in the days of Lancelot of The Lake, and the horses are sometimes painted to mimic the fancy livery that Sir Percival might have sported at a tournament in days of yore. The competition is colorful and lively.

The origins of this unique event in Ville Platte date back to the residency of Major Marcellin Garand, an officer in Napoleon's army, who moved to the central Louisiana town and established the tournament in the early 1800s. The tradition caught on but was, for some reason, lost to history and ended in the 1880s. In 1948, returning war veterans led by Judge J. D. Buller revived Le Tournoi as part of the Fourth of July festivities in Ville Platte.

In 1956 Le Tournoi was incorporated into the Cotton Festival, and it is now celebrated every October. Although this is when the official champion jouster is crowned every year, there are other such tournaments in the area. Still, the Louisiana legislature specified in 1958 that the championship must occur in Ville Platte.

The seven rings that are the focus of the jousters represent the seven enemies of cotton – hence the connection to the Cotton Festival. The seven enemies are: Flood, drought, the boll weevil, the bollworm, silk, rayon and nylon.

SWAMP POP MUSEUM

A musical genre that significantly influenced the wider music world

205 Northwest Railroad Avenue, Ville Platte
337-523-7206
facebook.com/people/Louisiana-Swamp-Pop-Museum/100057717210370
Fri & Sat 10am–3pm
Admission charge

Housed in a small red rectangular former railroad building in the heart of Ville Platte, the Swamp Pop Museum is a charming down-home museum dedicated to swamp pop, a rock and roll genre born on the Cajun prairie that arose in the late 1950s.

This musical genre, indigenous to the Acadiana region of south Louisiana and an adjoining section of southeast Texas, combines New Orleans-style rhythm and blues, country and western, and traditional French Louisiana musical influences. Its heyday lasted into the mid-1960s, when it was subsumed (like other rock-n-roll hybrids) by the so-called British invasion of American musical tastes.

The museum houses many objects, such as musical instruments and costumes, and a generous supply of posters, records and promotional materials donated by the stars. You'll also find lists of swamp pop greats and the hits they wrote and recorded, as well as knowledgeable docents who exhibit the famously friendly and open nature of Acadiana as they explain the genre and its importance.

What is swamp pop?

Swamp pop is a genre born from a melding of traditional Cajun and Creole music that came out of Acadiana and bled into south-east Texas. Influenced by Elvis Presley, Fats Domino, Bob Wills and Hank Williams, the musicians in Louisiana traded in their accordions and fiddles for electric guitars and saxophones. Some of the enduring hits of swamp pop that are still heard as regular offerings on oldies' radio include Bobby Charles's "See You Later, Alligator," covered by Bill Haley and the Comets; "Just a Dream" by Jimmy Clanton; "Sea of Love," by Phil Phillips; "I'm Leaving It Up to You" by Dale & Grace; and the more regionally recognized "Big Blue Diamonds" by Clint West. Many of the songs were first recorded by local and regional record labels such as Jin, Golden and Crazy Cajun. Swamp pop also significantly influenced the wider musical world: The Rolling Stones and The Beatles had hits that revealed the influence of the genre. However, one of the most famous rock-n-roll groups to be closely associated with swamp pop is Creedence Clearwater Revival, musicians who grew up in the San Francisco area, a far cry from the Bayou and Cajun prairies. John Fogarty penned songs like "Born on the Bayou" and "Fortunate Son" with strong swamp pop influences. Swamp pop still has a small number of passionate cult followers in the United Kingdom, Japan and northern Europe.

LOUISIANA ARBORETUM

A forgotten hiker's paradise

1300 Sudie Lawton Lane, Ville Platte
337-363-6289
lastateparks.com/parks-preserves/louisiana-state-arboretum
Daily 9am–5pm
Admission charge

Just 7 miles north of Ville Platte, in the center of the state, the Louisiana Arboretum is never even seen by the overwhelming majority of citizens.

Opened in 1961, it was the first state-supported arboretum in the South. It consists of 600 acres of natural-growth forest, with a few additional indigenous plants, so that almost every type of vegetation in the state can be found here. The only things missing are the coastal marsh and prairie plants. You're also likely to find an array of wood fauna such as deer, raccoon, skunks, possums, foxes and wild turkeys.

Inside the Nature Center, you'll find a detailed explanation of the trees, plants, flowers, fauna, and soils found here.

From the center it's a hiker's paradise, as there are five different marked trails so that you can enjoy the different trees all along the way. All the trails, which range from 0.2 miles to 1.5 miles in length, are rated either easy or moderate. Some hilly terrain is involved in the walks, but this is Louisiana, so "hilly" is a relative concept!

The Baldcypress Trail is a Cypress-Tupelo swamp on the edge of Chicot Lake and one of the more photo-worthy spots in the park.

The Paw Paw Loop, named for the Paw Paw tree, is hilly and runs through a Beech-Magnolia Forest.

The Walker Branch Trail, which is the longest at 1.5 miles, leads to the Caroline Dorman Lodge and the Walker Terrace (wheelchair accessible).

The Wetland Trail, over a vernal pool with a pavilion over the water, takes you to the lowest elevation of the park.

The Backbone Ridge Trail, which is 1.25 miles long and goes deeper into the forest than the others, has a pavilion, a covered bench and an overlook.

There is another entrance on Louisiana Highway 3042 with easy access to the Caroline Dorman Lodge, the Walker Terrace and Walker Branch Trail, as well as the Backbone Ridge Trail.

TUNICA-BILOXI CULTURAL AND EDUCATIONAL RESOURCES CENTER

One of the most advanced labs of its kind in the world

150 Melancon Road, Marksville
318-561-0400
tunicabiloxi.org
Mon–Fri 9am–noon and 12:30pm–4pm
Admission charge

Housed in an imposing orange-red building designed to resemble a 16th-century Tunica burial ground, the Tunica Cultural and Educational Resources Center is a 40,000-sq.-ft. facility that serves many purposes. It's a museum, a library, a meeting place, a center for tribal government and, not least of all, a world-class conservation and restoration laboratory.

Behind a large glass window, the laboratory can easily be viewed by visitors: It displays the modern expertise helping to preserve a fascinating past that can be traced back to Hernando de Soto's first glimpse of the Mississippi River. What you'll see is a scene from a CSI TV show. Scientists, archeologists, and technicians are restoring the Tunica Treasure, a collection of trade goods from the interaction between Native and European cultures between 1731 and 1764. The treasure represents an important link in preserving the Tunica-Biloxi tribal culture.

The facility and equipment here in Marksville are some of the most advanced in the world. Next to the laboratories, you'll find stacks of restored artifacts from the treasure.

The Tunica were a business-minded tribe that traded extensively with the French, Spanish, English and American settlers. You'll see a lot of 17th- and 18th-century ceramics and metal objects, such as cooking vessels, which have been restored in the lab.

Most of the treasured objects take around 18 months to restore. The finished effect strives for the 6–6 method: From up close, you can see that the item has been restored, but you can't tell from 6 ft. away.

The Tunica-Biloxi Museum gives a comprehensive overview of the complexity of the meetings of Native cultures with European newcomers … something you don't see very often.

Hernando de Soto arrived in the land of the Tunica on the Mississippi River in 1541 to great fanfare. There are three eyewitness accounts of this encounter here at the museum.

A fatal battle between the Natchez and the Tunica led to the death of the Tunica chief, Chauru-Joligo. His grave was discovered in the 1960s by a prison guard with a metal detector near Angola prison – it was this guard who unearthed the long-lost Tunica Treasure. The burial rituals of the Tunica included burying the goods and possessions of the deceased.

SARTO OLD IRON BRIDGE

The first Louisiana bridge to be put on the National Register of Historic Places

Bayou des Glaises
8554 Highway 451, Moreauville
318-997-2465

Along a remote, lazy country road, one of the least traveled in the state, stands a little-known steel truss swing bridge (a bridge that can rotate horizontally to allow ships to pass through), which has stood the test of time. A unique feat of engineering, it is one of the few swing bridges in the country. Built in 1916, the Sarto Old Iron Bridge was the first Louisiana bridge to be put on the National Register of Historic Places.

It is now a pedestrian bridge and can be reached by a serpentine concrete walkway. Below is a wooden observation deck, hovering over Bayou des Glaises, giving a good view of the structure or as a perch from which to fish. Bayou des Glaises is one of the many tributaries that flow into the Atchafalaya Basin.

The former Big Bend sits 5 miles from the Red River, 8 miles from the Mississippi, and 4 miles from the Atchafalaya, a strategic location for commerce as, back in the day, navigable rivers were the interstate highways of their time.

The occasional severe floods were problematic for life and property, however. Local citizens built the swing bridge not only to facilitate maritime river traffic but also as an escape route for both people and livestock. The floodwaters were sometimes so high that steamboats could pass through the usually shallow bayou.

In time, a nearby community, Naples, developed at the point where trains and boats could be loaded. The site became a significant railroad terminal. However, to show how dangerous the situation could become: One of the reasons to build swing bridges like the Sarto Bridge was the fact that Naples was washed away by the Great Mississippi River Flood of 1927. After this flood the levees were raised significantly, reducing the need for the Sarto Bridge.

The world's largest swing bridge is the El Ferdan Railway Bridge in Egypt, which spans the Suez Canal. The largest such bridge in the U.S. is the George P. Coleman Memorial Bridge at Gloucester Point, Virginia.

NEARBY
Adam Ponthier Grocery Museum
318-500-4036
Tours available Tue, Thurs & Fri 7:30am–3:30pm, Sun noon–4:30pm

Across the street from the bridge, the Adam Ponthier Grocery Museum offers tours of a well-preserved grocery store dating from the early 1900s. The museum contains a variety of artifacts such as mail, animal traps, and tools from the 1900s. It is a time capsule of mercantile wares. Closed in 1994, the Big Bend Post Office can also be visited at the grocery store. Big Bend was the name of the village that disappeared with the closure of the post office.

DRIVE-THROUGH FUNERAL HOME

Help at a difficult time

1018 Parent Street, New Roads
225-638-7544

On Parent Street in New Roads, it's difficult to guess what's inside what appears to be a recently closed bank – there might be a limousine parked under the overhang by the large picture window covered by a drape. What you're actually looking at is a drive-through funeral home.

At the beginning of the 21st century, America is increasingly becoming a drive-through society: Banks and fast-food restaurants have led the way. And in Louisiana, much to the amusement of people who visit the state from the outside world, locals are proud to call it the home of a genuinely indigenous enterprise: the drive-through daiquiri place.

The drive-through funeral experience is not unique to Louisiana – you'll find similar facilities scattered around the U.S. They pre-date Covid but were well suited to the challenges presented by the pandemic as the world tried to cling to as much normalcy as possible, even in an unnatural social landscape. Driving through in cars, in isolation from others, also prevented spreading the virus.

The drive-through funeral home serves a valuable purpose regarding the traditions and emotions involved in that special final right of passage. It allows people who are elderly, incapacitated, or unable to participate to come and pay their respects to their loved ones. This simple yet essential service can be helpful at a difficult time.

MISS JANE PITTMAN OAK

A literary reference?

11850 Louisiana Highway 416, New Roads

On Louisiana Highway 416, only a minute off of Louisiana Highway 1 and about 5 miles east of New Roads, in front of a residence near False River, stands a famous oak tree. The Miss Jane Pittman Oak and its 27-ft.-wide trunk was made famous by Ernest J. Gaines (a Louisiana native from Oscar) and his 1971 historical novel, *The Autobiography of Miss Jane Pittman*.

This oak (which Gaines says he walked by many times) is a key factor in Miss Pittman's recollections, which cover a varied life from her birth as a slave, the end of the Civil War, the life of a sharecropper in the Deep South, and historical events like the Great Flood of 1927 which had a huge impact on the northern migration of many African American citizens from areas like New Roads. The story stretches right into the Civil Rights movement of the 1960s.

In 1974 Gaines' novel became a TV sensation, starring Cicely Tyson as Miss Jane Pittman. The movie won nine Emmy awards. It was one of the first TV movies to treat African American characters in depth and with sympathy. It predated the blockbuster TV movie *Roots*, which also brought a new perspective to the subject of the struggles and lives of African Americans and introduced them to a wider audience.

Although the movie is based on Gaines' novel, its impact was bolstered by the fact that many people believed the story to be true.

In the novel, the oak is a symbol of rest, contemplation, community and remembering.

After a car ran into a branch that had fallen from the ancient oak onto the highway, the tree was in danger of being cut down as a safety measure. But the community (including Gaines himself) stepped in and the tree was saved: The Louisiana Department of Agriculture and Forestry had the tree inspected and found that it was indeed in fine health. However, you can clearly see today where the limbs were trimmed in order to preserve the integrity of the tree.

GRAVE OF GRACE AND SAM

27

The grave of two dogs who got married

40136 Louisiana Highway 942, Darrow
225-473-9380
houmashouse.com
Daily 9am–8pm
Admission charge

Near the entrance to the lovingly restored Houmas House Plantation, an elegant and tasteful grave has an interesting story to tell. The newly refurbished gravesite, lit at night to bring another dimension, is in memory of Princess Grace and King Sam, the beloved labradors of Kevin Kelly, the owner of Houmas House – they were married there in 2003.

On November 1, at an elaborate ceremony, Grace and Sam were married in front of a crowd numbering in the hundreds. King Sam was the first to arrive for the nuptials in a black horse-drawn carriage. He was attired in a tuxedo-like outfit.

Soon after Sam's regal entrance – to the delight of the crowd, who were waiting eagerly – Princess Grace arrived in her white horse-drawn carriage. The bride was resplendent in a white wedding dress and, from the enthusiasm she showed by eagerly jumping from her carriage when it came to a halt, was undoubtedly in the mood for the festivities.

The service was conducted in all seriousness, with Mr. Kelly next to his pets. It ended with the two lovebirds sealing the deal with a kiss.

Gospel singers on the second-story balcony serenaded the newly-weds and guests, and a reception with fine Louisiana cuisine and spirits followed, including a delicious wedding cake replicating the Houma House plantation house.

Princess Grace and King Sam have passed away, but they now spend eternity in the pet cemetery at Houmas House in the gorgeous gravesite.

Known as the crown jewel of River Road, Houmas House is now a tourist destination that showcases the splendor of the sugar plantations along the Mississippi River. It has the Great River Road Museum, a restaurant and other amenities. The film *Hush ... Hush Sweet Charlotte*, starring Olivia de Havilland and Bette Davis, was filmed here in the 1960s.

1811 SLAVE REVOLT TRAIL

28

America's First Freedom Trail

1811 Kid Ory Historic House, 1128 LaPlace
985 359 7300
Sat, Sun, Wed, Thurs and Fri 10am–3pm
By admission only

On the former site of the Woodlands Plantation, a trail was established in 2022 to commemorate the 1811 slave insurrection that some call America's first Freedom Trail. Inspired mainly by the successful slave uprising in Haiti (1791), the revolt started here at this house in LaPlace.

About 10 miles long, the trail travels from LaPlace over the Bonnet Carré Spillway and ends in Destrehan (in what is now Kenner), where, in

1811, a 500-strong group of slaves arrived on their way to the intended destination of New Orleans.

Each designated spot on the trail has an explanatory text that can be accessed via an audio tour that tells the story of the slaves from the perspective of their leader, Charles Deslondes. The audio is narrated by the actor Wendell Pierce, a native of New Orleans.

On January 5, 1811, Deslondes and other conspirators met to plan the endeavor. On January 8, hoping to use the Mardi Gras preparations as cover, they surprised plantation owner Colonel Manuel Andry, whom they awoke while armed with weapons. They wounded Andry and killed his son. They then gathered more participants, including maroons (former slaves who had fled and were living free in the swamp), as they moved down the river toward New Orleans. As word spread, the group was met by armed resistance from the planters.

With the news of the insurrection, Governor Claiborne tried to seal off the city and imposed a curfew on people of color. Eventually, the group led by Deslondes split into three after they were confronted by a militia led by General William Kempton. Deslondes was killed at the Jacques Fortier Plantation in what is now known as Kenner.

On January 13, the captured slaves were tried at a tribunal that lasted until January 15: Most were found guilty and executed. Many of the executed had their heads cut off and displayed on poles set into the levees for up to 60 miles around.

Tribunals were later held in New Orleans, and in these trials several of the insurrectionists were found innocent.

What is now known as the 1811 Kid Ory Historic House was once home to the legendary jazzman Kid Ory. It chronicles the career of this trailblazing jazz great who helped the music become a worldwide sensation. A commemorative text at the entrance to the house leads to three other sites that played a role as the slaves marched toward New Orleans. They are at Norco, Destrehan Plantation and the former Jacques Fortier Plantation in Kenner.

At the Whitney Plantation in Edgard, Louisiana, a powerful sculpture gives a chilling visual to the revolutionaries who took part in the quest for freedom: It depicts the heads of the condemned slaves on pikes.

FRENIER CEMETERY

29

The setting for a supernatural tale

110 Frenier Road, Laplace
504-467-0758
cajunprideswamptours.com
Daily 9:30am–4:15 pm

Under a canopy of trees on the edge of a swampy area where once a small town stood is a cemetery with a unique origin story. Here once stood Frenier. Today, if you want to see the place, you must take a tour and approach from the water. The remote spot does not disappoint as a setting for a supernatural tale and you'll have no trouble visualizing some powerful juju from your perch on the flat-bottom tour boat.

Julia Brown, a resident of Frenier, was quite a colorful character. She was a traiteur, a Cajun faith healer. Residents of the town would go to her to cure their ailments. As legend has it, they stayed away from her most of the rest of the time as she was also thought to be a voodoo priestess.

Ms. Brown, a Renaissance eccentric, was also an oracle. She had, over time, predicted more than a few disasters in other localities nearby,

and these prophecies had come to pass. She is said to have sat on her porch, guitar in hand, playing and singing songs. One of her lyrics, as the story goes, was: "One day, I'm going to die and take the whole town with me …"

There is no record as to whether the residents held their breath when she finally died but, as might be guessed, her funeral was well attended: No one in the community wanted to tempt fate or curry disfavor with Ms. Brown, even or perhaps especially from beyond the grave. On the day of her funeral, September 29, 1915, a Category 4 hurricane hit the New Orleans area. Only about 25 miles from New Orleans, the entire town of Frenier was wiped off the map.

Every resident of Frenier was killed save two. They moved out as soon as they could, leaving nothing of the town but the cemetery. The dead were buried in unmarked graves, with Ms. Brown's grave sitting perhaps 100 yards away from the others. (After a while, a fence and gravestone were placed to remember the other residents.)

Today, the land is surrounded by water. On your visit, you'll see a lot of gators but also raccoons, turtles, blue herons and herds of wild pigs who share the bayou landscape with the vanished town.

CHAPEL OF THE MADONNA

30

The smallest church in the world

28160 Louisiana Highway 405, Point Pleasant
Bayou Goula
map.ibervilleparish.com/listing/madonna-chapel/
Open 24 hours

Right there on Louisiana Highway 405, across the highway from the Mississippi levee, sits a large blue and white sign on a white wooden structure saying "The smallest church in the world." (It was chronicled once in a *Ripley's Believe it Or Not* newspaper feature.) If you blink as you pass through, you might miss it.

The Chapel of the Madonna of Bayou Goula is its proper name and, as one might guess, it is dedicated to the Virgin Mary. In a world that seems to be fueled by hype, this pint-sized house of worship delivers. One can envision a worshiper praying alone in the church and imagine the power of faith being focused in a way that might not be possible in a huge cathedral. There is an altar, a kneeler and numerous statues of Jesus, Mary and various saints; even a generous brace of devotional candles and holy cards.

The church was built by Anthony Gullo, a local sugar farmer. (Note that he was a simple farmer, not one of the more glamorous but infamous sugar planters, all members of the landed gentry.) When his eldest son fell seriously ill and was near death, Gullo (who was a devout Catholic) prayed fervently to the Blessed Mother for divine intervention: He promised that if his son recovered he would build a church in honor of the Blessed Virgin Mary.

The story had a happy ending: Gullo's son was cured, and with the land he donated and the help of neighbors who donated lumber, he built this fine little country church in 1903.

The church is billed as 8 x 8 ft. in some of the literature and 13 x 10 ft. in other accounts. The facade might suggest a square structure; the view from the rear would lead one to believe that the latter dimensions are probably more correct; nonetheless, it is still pretty intimate.

Every August 15 – Feast of the Assumption of the Blessed Virgin Mary – a mass is held here. On all other days of the year, the church is open for visitors to worship, light a candle, leave a donation for upkeep and perhaps ask for divine intercession for themselves or a loved one.

The key to the church is held in a key box so that anyone can enter. There is a visitors' log to mark that, indeed, you have been to the smallest church in the world on a country highway in Louisiana.

PLAQUEMINE LOCK STATE HISTORIC SITE

31

An impressive sight

57730 Main Street, Plaquemine
225-687 7158
lastateparks.com/historic-sites/plaquemine-lock-state-historic-site
Tue–Sat 9am–5pm
Admission fee

As you drive down Louisiana Highway 1 through downtown Plaquemine, you'll notice a unique building housing the Plaquemine Lock State Historic Site: The unusual Dutch-style structure, and its commanding presence right on the Mighty Mississippi, catch the eye immediately. It's an impressive sight, sitting above the deep lock that

was once the highest freshwater lift of any lock in the world, using a unique gravity flow principle.

The house stands next to the historic remnant of a lock that facilitated the commerce and population movement from the Mississippi River to Texas by way of the Atchafalaya Basin. It helped connect the commerce of the Mississippi by serving as a shortcut to southwest Louisiana and the Red and Atchafalaya Rivers.

Congress authorized the building of the lock in 1895 to facilitate the river commerce that was vital to the area around Baton Rouge and to the country. In 1925 this lock was the terminus for the Intercoastal Canal System linking much of the southeast via a navigable route. The lock was closed for good in 1961 after the Port of Greater Baton Rouge opened its new facilities at Port Allen.

Inside the museum are engineering exhibits which explain the science behind the concept of locks, and there are various models and bits of equipment that you can examine up close along with texts explaining the working of the lock together with photos from the days when the lock was in use.

You can stroll across a bridge and look down at the water and the concrete structures that once surrounded the lock: The size and depth are striking.

There is also a walkway that takes you up to the river for a close look at the Mighty Mississippi – this gives a good idea of the currents and the power that these locks had to deal with.

An open-air pavilion displays some of the boats and other water vessels that used the locks.

The same designer as the Panama Canal

The lock has the distinction of being designed by Colonel George W. Goethals, later the chief designer and engineer of the Panama Canal.

The lock house has been re-named the Gary J. Hebert Memorial Lock House in honor of the late Plaquemine publisher and editor who fought a four-year battle in the 1970s to save the structure and a portion of Bayou Plaquemine. At that time, city and state officials wanted to demolish the building and fill in the bayou to make way for a four-lane highway. Hebert was responsible for having the area put on the National Register of Historic Places, thereby saving it from demolition.

LAOTIAN BUDDHIST TEMPLE

An unexpected feast for the eyes

7913 Champa Avenue, Broussard
337-364-8078
wat-thammarattanaram-of-la-inc-at-new-iberia.hub.biz
Open 24/7

Just a short turn off of Louisiana Highway 90, in a well-maintained subdivision which at first glance could be anywhere in the U.S., you'll turn off of Melancon Street onto Vientiane Street and be greeted by a feast for the eyes: the totally unexpected sight of a Laotian Buddhist temple complex (Wat Thammarattanaram) in a community named Lanexang. The complex is so colorful and artistically rendered, and so chock-full of what could be called human skill and imagination, that it resembles a Mardi Gras float.

In the 1980s, after years of civil war, many Laotians immigrated to the United States and found themselves in disparate American communities. One of the places at which they landed was Broussard, a small town just south of Lafayette. The families (now numbering well over 1,000 people) pooled their money and bought the land that became Lanexang ('a million elephants'), named after the rich and powerful kingdom that was the center of Southeast Asian Buddhism for three and a half centuries (1353–1701). Work started on building the Buddhist complex in 1987.

The complex consists of a temple, a sermon hall, a drum pavilion, a statue pavilion, a makeshift crematorium and a sim (a building used for the ordination of monks). All the buildings are in classical Laotian architectural style, with a low brick wall separating the complex from the Lanexang residential area.

The entire temple complex is open all year but the *sim* is open to the public once a year only, to allow visitors to enter and receive blessings during the New Year's celebration.

A three-day festival

A three-day festival called Songkran is held between April 13 and 16 each year to celebrate the Laotian New Year – there are beauty contests, parades with floats that include religious elements and a raucous party much like Mardi Gras, with dancing, drinking and Karaoke singing. Visitors to the festival are welcome to receive a blessing from monks stationed at pavilions just for this purpose. The end of the festival has celebrants spraying each other with water hoses to signify cleansing for the new year.

Tours are available and the admission funds are used to send college students to Laos to continue their studies and give them a firsthand experience of their ancestral homeland.

TABASCO SAUCE
AT ST. JOSEPH CHURCH

A Cajun touch to the Last Supper

St. Joseph Church, Parks – 1034 Bridge Street
337-845-4168
Call ahead: office open 9am–1pm

Inside St. Joseph Church in Parks, a painting of the Last Supper may surprise the attentive observer: In front of Jesus, to his right, between a chalice and a wine decanter, if you look closely, you will recognize a bottle of Louisiana's iconic Tabasco sauce.

Done by local artist Christie Hebert, the painting is hung about 20 ft. in the air and attached to an arch, so it's rather difficult to see those small details. In fact, even the new pastor was unaware of the bit of humor residing in his church.

Everything started when Shane Bernard, the historical curator of the McIlhenny Company, began to hear a persistent rumor that there was a bottle of their iconic sauce in a religious painting in Parks. He sent a gently probing letter to the pastor of St. Joseph Church, Nicholas DuPré, inquiring about it. The new pastor, not knowing the answer, had to bring in a 12-ft. ladder to reach the arch from where the painting is hung.

It turns out that in around 2003, the then pastor, Rev. Bryce Sibley, thought the church needed a little art to spice up the decor. He commissioned Hebert to paint the Last Supper, asking her to add a local touch to the scene.

OAK AND PINE ALLEY

The amazing "road flanked by trees"

St. Martinville
Intersection of Louisiana Highway 96 (Catahoula) and Pine Alley Drive

Standing out in a flat rural agricultural area just a few minutes from downtown St. Martinville, a tunnel of tall oak and pine trees flanked by two large sugarcane fields makes an amazing sight that should not be missed.

Indicated by a historical marker at the junction of Louisiana Highway 96 (also called Catahoula Highway) and Pine Alley Drive ("the road flanked by trees"), the alley of trees is close to the Bayou Teche.

Initially, the trees are said to have been planted from the Teche toward the home of sugar planter Charles Durand around 1829 over a whopping 3-mile distance. Today only about a half mile of the alley remains but the effect is still exciting.

Durand came to the St. Martinville area in 1820 and was described as a bon viveur, a lover of life, and an original who often did the unexpected ... like planting those rows of trees.

The most spectacular wedding in the history of Louisiana

According to the tale which has been chronicled in the New York Times and Reader's Digest over the years, Durand wished to give his two daughters a double wedding that would be the most spectacular in the history of Louisiana.

To that end, he imported spiders from China and had his slaves climb up into the trees with bellows filled with gold and silver dust he had brought in from California. He sprayed the cobwebs, creating a surreal effect for the wedding party and the reported 2,000 guests. Another account says that the carriages carrying the couples were decorated with spiderwebs and gold dust. By all accounts, it was indeed one of the most memorable weddings in Louisiana and the entire South.

The wedding was recreated in 1955 on the bicentennial of the French expulsion from Canada by the English. Organizers sought a couple who would adjust their plans and be wed under the trees with the requisite cobwebs and precious metal dust. In this reenactment, the canopy was described as a gauze-like fabric extending 40 or 50 ft. into the air and heavily sprinkled with shimmering gold and silver dust.

LOURDES GROTTO REPLICA

Built by a free man of color

St. Martin de Tours Church – 133 Main Street, St. Martinville
337-394-6021
Mon–Thurs 9am–4pm (excluding daily Mass times: check ahead)
saintmartindetours.org

nside the beautiful St. Martin de Tours Church, known as the Mother Church of the Acadians, to the left as you face the altar, is a replica of the Grotto at Lourdes, in France, where the Blessed Mother appeared to Bernadette Soubirous in 1858.

The grotto is the creation of a free man of color, Pierre François Hyppolite Martinet, in the 1870s or 1880s. An architect and builder,

Martinet saw a postcard of the Lourdes Grotto. He used it as a guide to build the enduring shrine that now has many heartfelt thanks from parishioners for answered prayers sprinkled on the grotto.

The grotto is built out of bousillage, a common material found in old buildings in Acadiana: a mixture of Spanish moss, clay, mud, animal hair and vegetation, used as infill between timbers and half-timbered buildings.

Today, the shrine has a modern feel to it, but it is adorned with declarations and tributes to Mary that are 100 years or older. Many of them say simply 'Merci.'

Brochures in both English and French testify to the strength of the attachment to the French heritage that still thrives in Acadiana even some three centuries after the arrival of the French settlers. The Acadians, expelled from Nova Scotia by the English, arrived here in 1765 and the church was established in 1766.

The parish's history goes back to June 5, 1756. On that day, Fr. Pierre Didier performed the first ritual in the parish, which was to baptize Jean dit Ingui and Marie, two slaves, and then marry them. Fr. Didier baptized several other slaves on that same day.

The early history of St. Martin de Tours is a history of the Acadian settlement of the area. The church became the focal point around which a commercial district grew up, with many historical buildings still within easy walking distance.

Le Petit Paris

St. Martinville was once called 'Le Petit Paris' because many refugees from the French Revolution settled there and the town became known as a focal point for French customs and culture. After the founding of New Orleans, that city was beset with epidemics and people moved out in search of a healthier environment. St. Martinville, at that time, had fine hotels, a French opera house and a flourishing cultural scene.

Pierre François Hyppolite Martinet's family has quite a history. His relatives have played a key role in many events not only in and around St. Martinville but throughout Louisiana. His brother was a lawyer and physician in New Orleans and a member of the Comité des Citoyens, which funded the landmark Supreme Court case Plessy v. Ferguson in 1896.

CYPRESS SAWMILL COLLECTION

Memories of the cypress logging industry in south Louisiana

118 Cotton Road, Patterson
985-399-1268
louisianstateamuseum/org/museum/
wedell-williams-aviation-and-cypress-sawmill-museum
Tue–Sat 9:30am–4pm

The Cypress Sawmill Collection is a beautifully presented museum that chronicles the cypress logging industry in south Louisiana. As well as showcasing the ingenuity of the 20th century, it reveals humans' voracious appetite for the Earth's resources.

Airplanes, tractors, cypress-wood canoes that are hundreds of years old and an assortment of strange machinery fashioned especially to suit the unique needs of harvesting the bald cypress forests are found in a well-lit hangar-sized room.

There is an 800-year-old hollowed-out cypress log, a cypress cistern you can walk into and a vintage film taken over a century ago that illustrates how steam-powered engines accelerated the clearing of the cypress forests – by the 1960s, they had been all but decimated as a commercial enterprise.

"The wood eternal"

Called in promotional material "the wood eternal," the bald cypress has remarkable properties. In 2012 a submerged cypress forest of 53,000 years of age, fully intact, was found off the coast of Alabama. When the newly cut logs were brought up and examined by experts, they still gave off their distinctive aroma.

As early as 1699, French merchants at Biloxi were selling cypress for export to the French East Indies. In the 1700s, two-man teams of loggers would brave the swamp and cut down giant trees while balancing on small pirogues. They then assembled rafts to be moved through creeks, bayous, and rivers to either the Mississippi or, more likely, to the sawmills that were popping up in the area where the museum now stands.

The plumbing of New Orleans in the early years depended on cypress trees, known for their excellent waterproofing qualities. In 1915 a plumber working for the Sewage and Water Board (the New Orleans water agency) was upgrading the system: he was amazed to uncover the 250-year-old cypress pipes, which were still in excellent shape, not rotted or deteriorated.

The Cypress Sawmill Collection is part of the Wedell-Williams Aviation & Cyprus Sawmill Museum (see p. 168): Harry P. Williams was the scion of the Williams family who owned the large sawmill operation. His wealth was instrumental in funding the aviation feats chronicled in the aviation museum.

WEDELL-WILLIAMS AVIATION MUSEUM

37

The fastest woman pilot in the world

118 Cotten Road, Patterson
985-399-1268
louisianastatemuseum.org/museum/wedell-williams-aviation-and-cypress-sawmill-museum
Tue–Sat 9:30am–4pm

A fighter jet poised as if taking off on Louisiana Highway 90 at Patterson marks the location of a beautifully designed museum dedicated to two local men who were instrumental in the development of air travel.

Jimmy Wedell and Harry Williams were true aviation pioneers. They took the flying world by storm in the 1930s and helped to move air travel into the future with their expertise, passion and bravery.

As its centerpiece, the museum has several meticulously put-together replicas as well as original 1930s racing planes, some of which are the planes that set world speed records with Jimmy Wedell at the controls.

The planes are nothing less than stunning. You can go up close and investigate the cramped cockpits where the intrepid flyers risked their

ives in a quest for speed. The huge and powerful engines that propelled these planes into the record books are also on display: The size of these engines on the relatively small planes shows how dangerous this enterprise could be.

Memorabilia of the feats and triumphs and a children's interactive exhibit add a historical and educational element to the experience.

A film presentation in 4D is one of the most fun things in the museum: It brings the viewer back to the 1932 Cleveland Air Show at which the Wedell-Williams planes excelled and highlights the exploits of a Wedell-Williams team member, aviator Mary Haizlip. Haizlip was one of the top competitors in the races and, for three to four years in the 1930s, held the world record speed for female aviators. She was considered the fastest woman pilot in the world.

Sadly, both Jimmy Wedell and Harry Williams perished in plane crashes.

After Williams' death, his wife Margaret sold the air service company they had built to a company that eventually became Eastern Airlines, once one of the largest airlines in the world.

The aviation museum is coupled with a Cypress Sawmill Museum (see p. 166) in the same modern building, but each museum stands alone and deserves its own entry.

38

MR. CHARLIE
AT THE RIG MUSEUM

The world's first transportable, submersible, offshore drilling rig

111 1st Street, Morgan City
985-384-3744
rigmuseum.com
Tours (60 to 90 minutes): Mon–Sat 10am and 2pm
Admission fee

The world's first transportable, submersible, offshore drilling rig, Mr. Charlie rises 40 or more feet upon its derrick on a platform towering over the banks of the Atchafalaya River in Morgan City.

A truly groundbreaking development, the rig was deployed in 1953 near the mouth of the Mississippi by Shell Oil and remained in use until 1986. After more than 30 years of sucking oil out of the depths of the Gulf, it was retired and offered to the Smithsonian Institution. The Smithsonian had to turn down the historic structure because it was too large for them to accommodate.

Now it sits as a museum, looking like a well-worn industrial site blending in with the landscape of industrial activity that predominates this southern Louisiana city that is a hub of the offshore business. Historically, the success of Mr. Charlie led to a boom in the entire offshore oil drilling industry.

The deployment of the rig was worthy of a spread in LIFE magazine in 1954 – the article claimed that Mr. Charlie could drill a 12,000-ft. hole at a different location every month, and indeed over its lifetime it drilled over 200 oil and gas wells.

Designed by Alden "Doc" Laborde, the rig was initially spurned by all the major oil companies. No one wanted it. Laborde made the decision to search for investors and eventually found a partner in Charles Murphy, the owner of an independent oil company from El Dorado, Arkansas.

The groundbreaking oil rig was built at Alexander Shipyards in New Orleans, and it provided an alternative to the permanent pile-supported oil drilling of the time. As Mr. Charlie could be easily moved around, it was a game-changer.

For a brief time, Mr. Charlie was rivaled by another rig of similar design known as Mr. Gus, but Mr. Gus was destroyed by bad weather, which revealed how dangerous such an endeavor could be. Mr. Charlie survived until it had outlived its usefulness, but only after a long and distinguished record of success.

PETER PAN HOUSE

39

A reminder of the clubhouse of Peter Pan in Neverland

2206 Louisiana Highway 308, Raceland
Best seen from Louisiana Highway 1, bayou side, for unintrusive photos
Approx. 6.6 miles west of intersection of Louisiana Highway 182
or 7.7 miles east of Louisiana Highway 20
Private residence

On Bayou Lafourche near Raceland, a haphazard collection of architectural elements might at first look like a pile of random junk. Yet this is the home and creation of artist Juliana Martin and her husband, Lance Martin. Known as the Peter Pan House, it reminds people of the clubhouse of Peter Pan in Neverland. The singular structure is best seen from across Bayou Lafourche on Louisiana Highway 1, the backyard of the home.

Started in 2004, it is a work in perpetual progress. Juliana says she has an inordinate amount of creative energy, and she needs an outlet for it. She is the artist in residence and her husband supplies the carpentry skills.

The house includes (among other things) hundreds of miscellaneous pieces of bric-a-brac, numerous salvaged windows and cypress doors, many from New Orleans, as well as an abundance of wooden shutters, mantles, doors and Victorian architectural curlicues.

The backyard consists of connected slides (eight in all), various bits of playground equipment, multiple decks, boardwalks, trampolines, hammocks, tug boat ropes, tunnels, a barge tethered to a boat launch, several road signs, an old fire hydrant, and perhaps the most distinct and most talked-about feature: water slides saved from defunct water parks in nearby Houma.

The water slide that leads to the brown waters of Bayou Lafourche led to rumors that the Martins were opening a water park. But when the authorities came by to investigate, they just found a unique home.

The property has had to be expanded to accommodate the couple's growing children, and daughter Avah and son Tolan have what many kids would consider dream bedrooms. Avah has a slide that leads down from an elevated bed, and Tolan has a tunnel in his bedroom that leads toward the bayou and gives him a vantage point from on high to survey the unique backyard.

As to the genesis of the Peter Pan House, Juliana says it was simply that the family moved in and started doing what they do. Basically, "just what came to mind," according to the couple.

A wooden dwelling serves as Juliana's office and brainstorming space. The interior is illuminated by Christmas lights, wooden carvings, paintings and statues, and a few other things such as her office chair (a wheelchair).

People often ask the Martins, "Why?". To which Juliana answers, "Why not?"

MEMORIAL TO SEAMAN FIRST CLASS FREDDIE FALGOUT

40

The first American military casualty of World War II

4484 Louisiana Highway 1, Raceland
lacajunbayou.com/about/visitor/-info

On Louisiana Highway 1, just off exit 215A near Raceland, in the parking lot of the Lafourche Visitor Center, stands a little-known memorial, dedicated in 2020: It remembers Seaman First Class Freddie Falgout of Raceland, considered by historians as the first American military casualty of World War II.

At the bottom of the memorial, a square metal plate was apparently taken from the ship on which Falgout served and perished in Shanghai, China, on the deck of the U.S.S. Augusta on April 20, 1937. The plaque was retrieved by one of Falgout's shipmates from a scrap heap at Mare Island Navy Shipyard, where the Augusta was being refitted in 1940, and was later presented to Falgout's younger brother.

The Augusta had sailed up the Whangpoo River on a mission to evacuate American citizens from Shanghai. The Chinese forces were fighting to defend their homeland against the invading army of the Imperial forces of Japan in a precursor to what would become World War II.

Eyewitness accounts of the incident claim that on the morning of August 20, the Japanese forces had dropped two shells about 50 yards from the Augusta, a tactic they regularly used to disrupt foreign shipping.

The day's work was done and the crew of the Augusta had just finished their evening meal and were preparing to wind down with a movie to be shown on a screen on deck. Then, in the words of Commander C. W. Shantz, 'There was a sudden, nerve shocking, out-of-nowhere intrusion! A blinding flash! A rush of air! Screams, a low moan!' A 1-lb. shrapnel shell had exploded on deck. Although seventeen sailors were wounded, Seaman Falgout was the only one to lose his life.

As the U.S. Navy was not initially sure whether the shells came from the Chinese or the Japanese, they did not retaliate but, according to Commander Shantz, it was a deliberate attack by the Japanese. President Franklin Roosevelt declared the incident 'an unfortunate accident' and promised that U.S. forces would remain close to Shanghai to evacuate any Americans in need.

Falgout was buried in Raceland, which at the time had a population of about 600. Over 10,000 people attended his funeral.

BIG SHRIMP BOOTS

41

A Cajun symbol thanks to the Duke of Wellington ...

114 Tourist Drive, Gray
Exit 202 off Louisiana Highway 90
985-868-2732
explorehouma.com
Daily 9am–5pm

Outside of the Tourism Welcome Center at Gray Louisiana, a 7-ft. 6-in. pair of shrimp boots, an avatar of Cajun culture, makes a perfect photo op for tourists looking for a souvenir of their trip down on the bayou. The boots display a very south Louisiana symbol and the Cajun propensity to make fun of themselves.

A recognizable symbol to Louisianians, the boots are a staple of shrimping and fisherman design, yet they do serve a purpose: They keep your feet dry and perhaps afford a safe foothold so you won't fall off the boat.

Shrimping is a thriving way of life in this part of the world and has a documented history as an entrepreneurial endeavor going back as far as a report by the French explorer Le Page du Pratz in 1774. The industry pumps millions of dollars into the economy of Louisiana.

Among playful nicknames for the white boots are Cajun Reeboks, Chalmette Nikes, and Cocodrie Converse. You will even find beauty queens wearing them at pageants or they might appear in miniature as a Mardi Gras throw. The boots are a sure sign of the link to the local zeitgeist.

Yet, the origin of the design of the modern shrimp boot – adapted to make it easy to kick off if you fall into the drink (as it might be problematic to swim in waters teeming with alligators) – has a far-reaching historical connection.

The year was 1817, and the celebrated British war hero the Duke of Wellington tasked his personal shoemaker to design a boot based on the Hessian boot. Hoby, the shoemaker, streamlined the boot, and the fashion caught on in Britain. The upper class wore the new Wellington boot, which you may know as a "wellie."

In 1852, Charles Goodyear patented a process to vulcanize rubber in the manufacture of tires. A gentleman named Hiram Hutchinson purchased the patent with the idea of using it to make boots. Hutchinson, an American, opened his footwear manufacturing plant in France under the name A l'Aigle, which references the American Eagle. At the time, all agricultural workers in France toiled in the fields in wooden clogs. Soon everyone was plying their trade in rubber boots, keeping their feet drier and healthier.

In the trenches during both World Wars, the British army ordered the Wellington boots for its soldiers. Sometime in the years following World War II, the rubber boots – the forerunners of today's Cajun Reeboks – became a staple of the fishing industry.

DWIGHT EISENHOWER'S AIR FORCE ONE

42

The smallest plane ever used as Air Force One

Regional Military Museum
1154 Barrow Street, Houma
985-873-8200
regionalmilitarymuseum.com
Mon–Fri 10am–4pm, Sat 10am–2pm

At the center of one of the exhibition rooms at the Regional Military Museum in Houma, an Aero Commander 680 twin-prop plane built in 1956 sits with the words "Air Force One" prominently proclaimed.

This was the plane that President Dwight Eisenhower used for short flights that did not require a large aircraft. Eisenhower, a pilot, loved to fly the plane himself, mostly on flights to his home town of Gettysburg or to Camp David, the famous presidential retreat he renamed after his grandson.

The plane, which may be examined from up close, was used until Eisenhower's term ended in 1961 and today it seems extraordinary that a U.S. president was squired around in what by today's standards is a very small aircraft. Measuring approximately 35 x 14 ft. with a 44-ft. wingspan, the plane weighs in at 4,200 lb. As such, it was the smallest plane

ever utilized as Air Force One. It could accommodate eight passengers and was equipped with a bed after Eisenhower suffered a heart attack.

The plane's flight log is on display at the Regional Military Museum and visitors are welcome to thumb through it. One of Eisenhower's passengers noted in the log is Field Marshal Bernard Montgomery, commander of the British Eighth Army during World War II.

The plane was taken out of presidential service in 1960 and bounced around since then before landing in Houma. For a time, it was used by the civil air patrol in Nebraska and then as a parachute jump training vehicle at the Air Force Academy. It eventually ended up at the Wedell-Williams Aviation & Cypress Sawmill Museum in Patterson. When the museum expanded and modernized, the plane was loaned to the museum in Houma in 2010. The back wall had to be removed to accommodate the 44-ft. wingspan: As the wing is made from one piece, it couldn't be removed.

The rest of this very fine museum has an extensive display relating to all the conflicts of the 20th and 21st centuries.

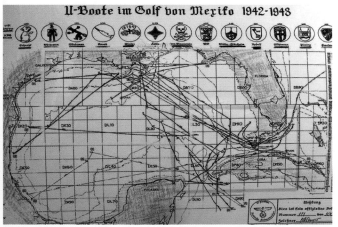

German U-boat map of U-boat activity in the Gulf of Mexico in World War II.

Two Air Force Ones in the air at the same time

Few people know that there are two Air Force Ones: At any given time, when the U.S. president is in flight, there are two planes in the air to foil any foul play. But this model plane was the first to have the blue-and-white painted emblem still used today on the outside of Air Force One.

MANDALAY NATURE TRAIL

43

The unique geographical pleasures of southern Louisiana

3599 Bayou Black Drive, Houma
985-853-1078
explorehouma.com/blog/post/explore-mandalay-nature-trail

Off the beaten path down a gravel road off Louisiana Highway 182, you'll find a short 0.9-mile nature trail that brings you up close to the unique geographical pleasures of southern Louisiana. The walk on a very peaceful boardwalk takes about 15 minutes round trip unless you decide to linger and take in the natural beauty.

Once you get to the overlook, you may want to soak up the unique area and perhaps bird watch. It's a great spot for waterfowl observation

and you might even see a bald eagle soaring above you. The Mandalay Wildlife Refuge, which can be seen at the end of the nature trail, provides a critical spring and fall neo-tropical habitat for migratory waterfowl and as such is a great place to bird watch.

Along the way to the refuge, under the Spanish moss-draped canopy trees such as oak, gum, cypress, tupelo and palmetto, you may also see an array of wildlife such as an alligator or two, turtles, armadillos, crawfish, nutria, snakes and probably a few bugs.

Mostly, though, it's a serene landscape and an easy walk into nature.

A trembling prairie

The Mandalay Wildlife Refuge covers over 4,212 acres and was established in 1996 to conserve and protect the freshwater marsh of West Terrebonne Parish. The refuge is a mix of freshwater marsh, cypress-tupelo swamp, and manmade canals, and it bisects the Gulf Intracoastal Canal.

There is also a unique habitat at the refuge that is found in only a few places on earth: the flotant marsh, or floating marsh. It is also called the 'prairie tremblante', or trembling prairie, as it is a floating mat of vegetation not anchored to the soil and is often sturdy enough for a person to stand on. Other places in the world where this floating marsh may be found are the papyrus swamps of the White Nile and the Amazon.

CHINE NET SHOP

44

See how the shrimping industry's nets are made, with typical Cajun hospitality

1901 N Bayou Drive, Golden Meadow
5am–5pm, but days may vary. Call ahead
985-475-6788

Along Bayou Lafourche in Golden Meadow, Chine Net Shop is actually more than a shop: It's also a place where you can see how the shrimping industry's nets are made in what, sadly, may be another vanishing sight of Louisiana's unique culture.

The shop was opened by Lawrence "Chine" Terrebonne in 1966 and then moved to its present location in an old supermarket building. Chine started working with his father in the shrimp net business when he was nine, and he's still vibrant and friendly into his eighties.

You can walk in and take a look and even get a demonstration as to how they do it. Best to call ahead if you'd like a deep dive although they're very friendly and welcoming if you just walk in.

When Chine started, the nets were made of cotton and needed to be dried in the sun to prevent rotting. But as of the 1950s, nylon replaced cotton, and in 1960, polyethylene was added to the materials used.

The front of the shop is a long, well-lit room with green netting displayed on all sides, waiting for pickup by customers, and supplies a one of-a-kind visual. You'll probably find men speaking French sitting or working in the room, and they'll be glad to let you look around and answer any questions.

Out back, you'll find the men who fashion the nets, and you'll see the larger, heavier and thicker netting used not in the shrimping business but in the offshore oil business. These coarsely woven green nets (which, to the uninitiated, may look like larger versions of the shrimping nets in the front of the shop) are called gorilla nets and now supply the lion's share of the income for Chine's Net Shop.

The gorilla nets are used for environmental mitigation. When an oil rig is decommissioned, the oil company must take the equipment away, and the rigs create quite a bit of iron and cement debris. The nets capture the larger items left behind, and then a sample net is raked over the area from each direction, with several sweeps until all the debris is gone.

KENNY HILL SCULPTURE GARDEN ㊺

A folk-art masterpiece

5337 Bayou Drive, Chauvin
For information or to arrange a tour of the site, call the Nicholls State
University Art Studio at 985-594-2546 or the Nicholls State University Division
of Art at 985-448-4597
nicholls.edu/folkartcenter/park.html

At the end of a quiet, suburban residential road on the banks of Bayou Lafourche, a concrete sculpture garden has been created from the vision of one man, Kenny Hill, a Vietnam vet. It is nothing short of a folk-art masterpiece.

It took Kenny ten years to create. Although hurricane winds have knocked down a few of the statues, the garden now has more than 100 life-size figures, including many of a religious nature: numerous angels, many winged creatures, several depictions of Jesus and a large concrete tower that has many allusions to American culture, some subtle, others not.

The garden, which is a riot of symbolism and whimsy, more than lives up to its press clippings. It was voted one of the twelve finest examples of folk art in the world. Its remote location, however, keeps most people from ever seeing it.

People who were initially skeptical about the new neighbor who had moved in and started building his eccentric concrete figures at a relentless pace have said that Kenny was a real down-to-earth guy who just wanted to enjoy the simpler things in life. His opus on the bayou is anything but simple. He has told artists and art professors and anyone who asked that he does not have an interpretation of his work and hopes that everyone who sees the statues and garden will have their own personal view of their meaning.

He told Southeastern Louisiana University art professor Dennis Sipiorski that he would never think of selling any of his art because he would lose his ability to create. Kenny was a rare breed indeed.

At some point the landlord had him evicted from the property for not keeping it up. Kenny soon vanished, and no one knows where he is now.

In order to save this unique wonder, Professor Sipiorski asked the owners of the property to give him two weeks to find a buyer. He contacted the Kohler Foundation, who have saved other folk-art sites around the state of Wisconsin. Someone from the foundation flew down to Louisiana to take a look and agreed to save Kenny Hill's masterpiece. They also bought an adjacent lot for events as well as the property across the street to serve as a welcome center. The foundation then turned it over to Nicholls State University in nearby Thibodaux, whose art department is now charged with its upkeep.

OUR LADY OF THE SEA STATUE

A beacon to mariners

8249 Redfish Street, Cocodrie

Iigh above a weathered wooden piling at the end of Highway 56, at the junction of Bayou Petit Caillou and the Houma Navigable Canal at Cocodrie, a surprising sight awaits visitors: a statue of the Virgin Mary. In 1958, the Rodeo Association put a beacon on Isle Dernière ('Last Island') to inspire fishermen on their way out to sea and welcome them home.

The area is overwhelmingly Catholic, and as you drive toward Cocodrie, you'll see many tributes to the Virgin Mary in the front yards and porches. These tributes often take the form of something called a bathtub Virgin: grottos made from bathtubs buried in the ground with a statue of Mary inside. So the decision to put the Virgin Mary on a large pyramid on Isle Dernière seemed an obvious choice.

However, it became clear that the barrier islands, including Isle Dernière, were living on borrowed time as erosion and climate change encroached, with the sea claiming over 25 sq. miles of land every year.

Erosion in coastal areas is not a new phenomenon in this part of the world. Isle Dernière was once a large resort that catered to the burgeoning middle and upper class of New Orleans. In 1856, a Category 4 hurricane with 155 mph winds destroyed the resort, and over 200 people lost their lives.

In more recent times, with the barrier islands slowly disappearing, it became clear that the statue of Mary had to be moved. The pyramid was abandoned and in 1982 the statue was placed atop a 60-ft. piling at a new location. In 2014 the statue was moved again to its present location.

Made from Carrara marble by Italian sculptor Aldo Perna, the 6-ft. statue of the Blessed Mother had a plaque added in 2002 that says: "In celebration of God's gift of our members and our coastal resources."

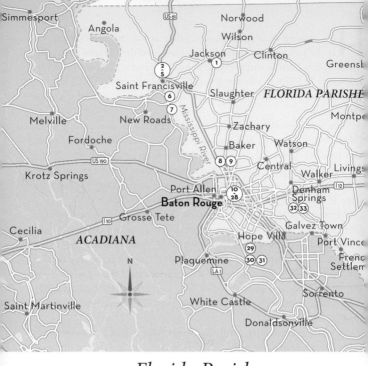

Florida Parishes

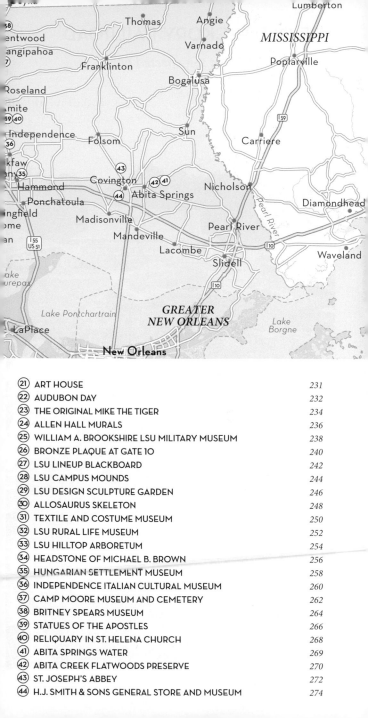

THE OLD HICKORY RAILROAD

A wonderland in an unexpected place

3312 College Street, Jackson
225-634-7397
louisianasteamtrain.com
2nd and 4th Sat of the month: 10am–2pm

Right on College Street (named after the fact that Centenary College was first situated here), just two blocks from Louisiana Highway 10, you'll find an extraordinary pathway back to your childhood or just an amazingly playful situation that probably appeals to the child in every one of us: a model train wonderland in an unexpected location.

Up on the hill where the Republic of West Florida Historical Museum is situated, this little gem of an outdoor model train display is complete with trucks, railroad cars, tunnels, trestles and miniature buildings from the heyday of railroads in one of the most skillfully put-together setups you will likely see anywhere.

This miniature world is the creation of the Greater Baton Rouge Model Railroaders, a non-profit organization that has been in existence for over 20 years.

The beautiful outdoor train display, often landscaped with real plants, including what appear to be sculpted bonsai trees, is only scratching the surface of this attraction.

Inside the several buildings of the Republic of West Florida Museum is a galaxy of model trains with up to seven layouts at any given time. Everything from O, H, S, G gauge, N, HO and even a Z scale, which, for those not in the know, is the smallest model train size.

There are up to five complete track systems, each equipped with all the bells and whistles of model railroading. There are track switches, bridges, water towers and train cars of every description and color as well as buildings, train depots and small "humans" to give a sense of scale (some appear to be in poses that add to the sense of whimsy).

Twice a month (see opposite), train enthusiasts are there to explain the gamut of the model train world: the setups, the gauges, the history of the different companies and all the whys and wherefores of model training. The non-profit also teaches about real railroading and explains how this practical, yet romantic transportation system works in the real world.

Another feature is a special setup to accommodate model steam train engines: You can see them in action as well, with a view of the technology that hurtled the U.S. into the future over 175 years ago.

You can learn model making, model landscaping, how to make realistic scenery and how to build your own miniature railroad. You can also bring your own model train cars and equipment and get instruction on how to get them rolling again.

FLAG OF THE REPUBLIC OF LOUISIANA

An independent country for about two weeks in 1861

West Feliciana Historical Society Museum
11757 Ferdinand Street, St. Francisville
225-635-6330
westfelicianamuseum.org/
Daily 10am–4pm

At the West Feliciana Historical Society Museum, as in various obscure places in Louisiana, an unfamiliar, distinctive flag hangs in the middle of the other more recognizable flags flown over the state. It's the flag of the short-lived Republic of Louisiana – Louisiana was technically an independent country for about two weeks in 1861.

On January 26, 1861, by a vote of 117 to 17, Louisiana declared independence from the United States. This was, of course, a prelude to Louisiana joining the Confederate States of America.

Many of Louisiana's citizens celebrated the separation from the Union. There was a parade of torch-bearing citizens in New Orleans; cannons and fireworks heralded the event that had been simmering for years over the issue of slavery. The governor of Louisiana asked people to leave lights on in their windows to commemorate and support the action.

Of course, a new country needed a new flag. The flag that flew over the Republic of Louisiana for two weeks, as the state finally joined the Confederacy on February 4, 1861, is a colorful one. There are 13 horizontal stripes, one for each of the original 13 colonies. The colors red, white, and blue are a tribute to the French tricolor. At the left-hand upper corner, a square red field has a large gold star – an acknowledgment of Spanish rule over Louisiana, as red and gold are the colors of the Spanish flag.

Another unusual flag is sometimes seen in Louisiana: the Bonnie Blue flag of the Republic of West Florida (see p. 198).

You can also find a flag of the Republic of Louisiana hanging at Mansfield Women's College, and another one in the Hall of Fame at the Louisiana Country Music Museum in Marthaville, but it is unmarked.

THE BALD CYPRESS TREE AT CAT ISLAND NATIONAL WILDLIFE REFUGE

The world's largest bald cypress tree ... and still growing

Creek Road, 4.6 miles west of St. Francisville
985-882-2000 – fws.gov
Before visiting, check flooding conditions on the above website
St. Francisville Historical Society: 11757 Ferdinand Street, St. Francisville
225-635-4224

About 4 miles west of St. Francisville, at Cat Island National Wildlife Refuge, a bald cypress tree surrounded by cypress knees that are often taller than your average person is thought to be anywhere between 1,200 and 1,500 years old – by bald cypress standards, this could be considered middle-aged! Designated the official tree of Louisiana in 1963, and native to the southeast United States, the bald cypress is believed to live for up to 3,500 years or more.

Although not the oldest, this magnificent tree (the 6th largest in the United States) is the biggest tree east of the Sierra Nevada and the world's largest bald cypress: about 100 ft. high and 58 ft. in circumference, it is still growing.

It might be two trunks, but as it forks about 13 ft. up, it's hard to tell. These giant trees often split over time, and the way that experts check is the root system. Since this tree is a focal point of research, it's a good bet that it has only one root system. Big enough for you to stand in and take a photo, this twisty giant could be from the special effects department of a *Lord of the Rings* film.

The Cat Island National Refuge's mission is to conserve, restore, and manage one of North America's last naturally functioning bottomland forest habitats. It is also tasked with monitoring the vulnerability to climate change of the bald cypress swamps.

The 9,623-acre reserve is home to a wide variety of migrating fowl, endangered plants, and animals that call it home, including bobcats, minks and black bears.

How to visit the tree with the hard-to-predict flooding of the area

The tree at Cat Island can easily be visited if the Mississippi River and the surrounding Sara Bayou cooperate. The hard-to-predict flooding of the area encompassing the refuge makes it imperative to check ahead if you plan to visit. Levee systems do not protect the refuge and so floods are common. For a significant part of the year, the tree can only be reached by boat. The best bet is to check with the Friends of Cat Island National Wildlife Refuge or inquire at the St. Francisville Historical Society found on Ferdinand Street in St. Francisville. When the refuge is not flooded, the trail (which can be reached by car on an unpaved roadway) is a simple 0.8-mile trek back and forth.

A bald cypress in Black River, North Carolina, is believed to be about 2,700 years old.

SECRETS OF THE CEMETERY AT ST. FRANCISVILLE

'The Day the War Stopped'

11621 Ferdinand Street, St. Francisville
225-635-4065
gracechurchwfp.org
Mon–Fri 9am–2pm

In 1863, the Civil War was raging in this part of Louisiana. A few miles from St. Francisville, sitting near the bluffs of the Mississippi River, Port Hudson was the focal point of a vital siege and battle to control the Mis-

sissippi and Red Rivers. The Confederates had thwarted David Farragut's Union fleet from high on the bluffs, but two Union ships had gotten through the bombardment. They had used Grace Episcopal Church (an English Gothic-style church built in 1893) and St. Francisville for target practice. On June 12, 1863, the mood, at least briefly, took an unusual turn.

The commander of the Union vessel U.S.S. *Albatross*, Lt. Commander John E. Hart, was suffering from the ravages of yellow fever and, in the throes of delusion, took his own life. The *Albatross* guns fell silent. Under a white flag of truce, the executive officer of the ship, Theodore B. Dubois, approached the Confederates at St. Francisville and, much to their astonishment, asked if there were any Masons in the town. Dubois requested that Lt. Commander Hart be buried with full Masonic honors in the same cemetery that he had been bombarding.

As luck would have it, St. Francisville was home to the oldest Masonic Lodge in Louisiana. Captain William Walter Leake of the Confederate Army, who had been shooting at the *Albatross* and the other Union vessels, was the Senior Warden of Feliciana Lodge No. 31 and he was summoned to deal with the request.

The request was granted, and the war was halted for a full Masonic burial conducted by both Union and Confederate combatants. Ever since, this interlude of peace and brotherhood has been known as "The Day the War Stopped."

Every year, on the second Saturday in June, the event is recreated by Louisiana Lodge No. 31 and New York Masonic Lodge No. 6 of Schenectady, New York.

Leake, who later became Master of the St. Francisville Lodge, maintained Hart's grave and decorated it with flowers for the next 49 years, until his own death in 1912. Leake was buried near Hart, and the two former enemies are commemorated with a single marble slab, placed in 1955 by the Grand Lodge of the State of Louisiana and "dedicated to the universality of Freemasonry."

A mysterious tomb

There is a myth that Confederate soldiers hid in a mysterious tomb at the back of the cemetery. Other people say that the steps behind the heavy iron gate of this now-weathered brick structure, overgrown by vegetation, lead down under the ground to where a widower had a rocking chair to keep his beloved deceased wife company. Neither of these stories has any historical verification and there is no marker for anyone who might be buried here.

FLAG OF THE REPUBLIC OF WEST FLORIDA

An independent country for two months in 1810

West Feliciana Historical Society Museum
11757 Ferdinand Street, St. Francisville
225-635-6330
westfelicianamuseum.org
Daily 10am–4pm

The blue flag with one star that hangs in conjunction with the American flag in front of the West Feliciana Historical Society Museum represents something that most Americans have never heard of and it deserves more respect for a variety of interesting reasons. It is the flag of the Republic of West Florida, which was an independent country in the continental U.S. for two months in 1810.

A beautiful small town on the Mississippi River, St. Francisville was the capital of the little-known republic. Its flag – one of the flags of the Confederacy during the "War Between the States" – was almost as

popular as the "Stars and Bars" that most people recognized as the flag of the Confederacy.

In a building dating from 1888 that once housed a blacksmith's shop and later a hardware store, the museum displays, among other things, stories about John James Audubon, who started painting his *Birds of America* at nearby Oakley Plantation (see p. 232), and the eight flags that have flown over Louisiana and West Feliciana Parish.

The Republic of West Florida has a complex history for such a short-lived independent state. The story is broken down inside the museum, along with other interesting aspects of the history of the area surrounding St. Francisville.

The Bonnie Blue flag was created by Mrs. Melissia Johnson, wife of the commander of the assault on the Spanish fort in Baton Rouge. Today you might still see the blue flag with its one star hanging from buildings in the area.

For more information about the Republic of West Florida, see following double-page spread.

Another blue flag with a large white star hangs on the wall to your right as you enter the museum. Some say it was the model for the Lone Star flag of the Republic of Texas.

Gone with the Wind and the Republic of West Florida

In Gone with the Wind, Rhett Butler names his daughter Bonnie because she has eyes "as blue as the Bonnie Blue flag," the popular name for the flag of the Republic of West Florida.

The Republic of West Florida: a republic that was independent for 34 days

The Republic of West Florida was a short-lived independent republic founded on September 23, 1810. After just 34 days, the U.S. Government annexed the republic and incorporated it into the Territory of Orleans (the part south of the 33rd parallel of the former French Louisiana, which on April 30, 1812 became the 18th state of the Union under the name of Louisiana). The republic began east of the Mississippi, from north of Lake Pontchartrain to south of the 31st parallel, and extended west of the Perdido River, between Mobile and Pensacola. The southern border was the Gulf of Mexico. The former republic was later divided between the states of Louisiana (now Florida Parishes) in the far west (Baton Rouge region), Mississippi (Biloxi region), and Alabama (Mobile region). Historically, the West Florida region was split in two: The west belonged to Louisiana and France, the east to Spain, with the border between Mobile and Pensacola at the Perdido River. In 1762, following the Seven Years' War and the signing of the Treaty of Fontainebleau, France ceded the virtually deserted and unexplored Louisiana to Spain. In 1763, again following the Seven Years' War and the signing of the Treaty of Paris, the region (and all of Florida) came under British rule (although Louisiana remained Spanish). In 1783, following the independence of the United States, West Florida returned to full Spanish control (along with the rest of Florida). But at the end of the 18th century, with Napoleon Bonaparte taking power in 1799 and launching a new Italian campaign (1799–1800), Spain came under pressure from France and signed the secret Treaty of San Ildefonso (1800), under which Spain ceded Louisiana back to France. In exchange, Spain obtained the creation of the Kingdom of Etruria in Italy, which was dependent on Spain. With its South American colonies in trouble, Spain wanted to refocus on Europe, and Bonaparte foresaw the possibility of an American empire if the Saint-Domingue expedition succeeded in the West Indies, as well as a fallback base for the planters of Saint-Domingue in the event of failure. In either case, the secret treaty also facilitated the election of Napoleon's ally Thomas Jefferson to the American presidency, while the Federalist party, which had been in power until then, had formed an alliance against France with the Haitian revolutionary Toussaint Louverture. In 1803, Napoleon decided to sell Louisiana to the United States. He wanted to finance his expansionist policy in Europe, get rid of a virtually untouched and undeveloped territory that was of no value to him, and strengthen the ties of friendship that had bound France and the U.S. since the War of Independence. In theory, however, the sale excluded the eastern part of the Mississippi, which was attached to West Florida and remained part of the Spanish colonial empire: This part of the territory had not been clearly included in the Treaty of San Ildefonso (1800). But English speaking settlers were increasingly resentful of Spanish rule. Those in the Natchez District (north of Baton Rouge, in present-day Mississippi – on land that rose a little, sheltered from the Mississippi's floods) had become very wealthy from 1795 onwards, following a local adaptation of Eli Whitney's invention of the cotton gin, which boosted the productivity of cotton production and lowered its cost, opening up immense potential. But only if there was land on which to grow the cotton… And the eastern part of the Mississippi was the most attractive for growing cotton. In 1817, Spain decided (like the United States and in the wake of England) to abolish the slave trade. At the same time, French refugees were arriving en masse on all the southern coasts of the United States following the 1809 anti-French events in Saint-Domingue and Cuba. On September 23, the rebels overwhelmed the Spanish garrison at Baton Rouge and unfurled the flag of the new republic: a single white star on a blue background, a flag later named the Bonnie Blue Flag. As early as October 27, 1810, the western (ex-French) part of West Florida was nevertheless annexed by a proclamation issued by U.S. President James Madison, who claimed the region as part of the Louisiana Purchase. The United States took possession of St. Francisville on December 6, 1810 and Baton Rouge on December 10, 1810. These territories were incorporated into the newly created Orleans Territory, which became the State of Louisiana in 1812.

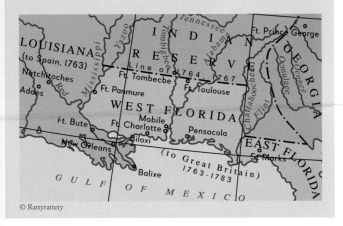

© Rattyrattery

HEMINGBOUGH

One of Louisiana's best-kept secrets in a completely unexpected spot

10101 Highway 965, St. Francisville
225-635-6617 – hemingbough.com
Open when there is no scheduled event

In a completely unexpected spot that is below the radar of most Louisianians, Hemingbough is a center for spiritual awareness and awakening set in a beautifully landscaped garden with statues of deer and mythological figures, a Roman pool and a breathtaking amphitheater. One of Louisiana's best-kept secrets, this totally unexpected classical landscaped garden is a true feast for the eyes: not to be missed.

Hemingbough is mostly an event venue (weddings, parties, theater, rock concerts, and opera and symphony performances) and has a small guest house offering bed and breakfast, but on days when there is no event, you are welcome to wander the grounds to take a peek.

The main attraction here are the grounds themselves, which have a romantic atmosphere and a notable European vibe, close to the Mississippi.

For many people, the visual highlight is the outdoor Greek amphitheater, which holds over 200 spectators seated on aluminum sculpted chairs with the sleepy Lake Audubon as a stunning backdrop. The amphitheater is also the site of the annual Hemingbough Easter Service.

The Edward Dease Memorial Chapel is a renovated 1902 post office that has been moved to the grounds.

A Buddhist shrine that survived the blast at Hiroshima during World War II

The manicured grounds of Hemingbough are home to a Japanese garden, a tribute to master gardener James Imahara, who created a beautiful garden in St Francisville. The garden also contains a stone shrine that survived the blast at Hiroshima during World War II. The Imahara family shrine was moved to the United States by Walter Imahara, James' son, with the blessing of Buddhist monks in Japan. It survived the blast at Hiroshima because it was on the side of a hill, which somehow protected it from destruction.

PORT HUDSON STATE HISTORIC SITE

A world-class historical museum at the site of the longest siege in U.S. military history

236 Louisiana Highway 61, Jackson
225-654-3775
lastateparks.com/historic-sites/port-hudson-state-historic-site
Daily 9am–5pm (closed Thanksgiving, Christmas & New Year's Day)
Admission charge (62 and older: free)

Alone Civil War vintage cannon marks the site of a world-class historical museum that sits just off Louisiana Highway 61 between Baton Rouge and St. Francisville. A small sign that blends in with the surrounding terrain is easily missed as you buzz down the road.

While you drive through the peaceful, almost cinematic forest dappled by sunlight, it's almost impossible to imagine the brutal events and significance of the battle that took place here in 1863.

The first thing you see as you emerge from the trees is a vast green plain surrounded by split rail fences and then the vintage Civil War cannons that point toward the open spaces of the battleground. You will also see the modern wooden building that houses the museum.

The grounds themselves are extensive. A 6-mile trail brings you from the museum and the parking area. You'll see more artillery, a few redoubts, strategic berms, Fort Desperate, and observation towers that give a bird's eye overview. From the extensive fortifications and logistics it took to fend off an attacking force, you'll get a feeling of what it might have been like to be there in a time of war.

Inside the museum there are many descriptive accounts of the battle and the men who fought here. You'll find beautifully crafted dioramas and artifacts such as stoves, personal belongings and weapons – for a small museum, it packs a lot of punch. There is an audiovisual presentation as well as guides and rangers to answer questions.

The Confederate Army chose Port Hudson for its geographic location after the fall of New Orleans to protect supply lines along the Red River, which were essential in supplying the heart of the Confederacy from Texas. Sitting on a prominent bend in the Mississippi, Port Hudson was the first highest bluff north of Baton Rouge: a perfect spot to defend against the Union Army's attempt to control the entire Mississippi.

The 48-day siege at Port Hudson, where 7,000 Confederates met a Union force of 30,000, was the longest siege in U.S. military history.

The Confederates were reduced to eating horses, rats and mules as they held out, but when word came of the fall of Vicksburg on July 4, 1863, Major General Franklin Gardner decided that the cause was futile and he surrendered Port Hudson five days later.

With the fall of Port Hudson, the Union Army controlled the entire length of the Mississippi River.

The first time that African American troops fought for the U.S. government

The Battle for Port Hudson was the first time that African American troops fought for the U.S. government. It was deemed an "experiment" at the time. After the battle, Port Hudson served as a recruitment station for African American soldiers. Every last weekend in March, there is a full reenactment of the battle at the park. The park and museum are maintained by the State of Louisiana.

THE RED STICK SCULPTURE

How Baton Rouge got its name

Leon Netterville Drive – Southern University, Scotlandville
225-578-6544 – subr.edu

On a bluff overlooking the Mississippi on the campus of Southern University, you'll find an abstract geometric sculpture designating the spot where history tells us how Baton Rouge got its distinctive name.

The Red Stick, by Frank Hayden, is a long red shaft pointing upward, surrounded by a futuristic Native American motif: It symbolizes the place where French Canadian explorer Pierre Le Moyne d'Iberville, sailing down the river in 1699, spotted a red stick planted by the Houma

and Bayagoula tribes to designate a boundary of their territories. The stick was covered in animal parts and the blood of animals fresh from the hunt. D'Iberville called the spot "red stick," which is how Baton Rouge got its name.

Southern's campus sits to the north of Baton Rouge on Scotts' Bluff, overlooking an unusual, unspoiled-by-modern-man view of the river. It's quite isolated geographically from the rest of Baton Rouge, technically in Scotlandville, with a guard post to enter the campus. Because of its location, most people in Baton Rouge – and certainly not visitors to the Louisiana capital city – will ever come across this statue by renowned sculptor and Southern professor, Frank Hayden.

Hayden was the foremost African American sculptor of the Civil Rights era. One writer described him "as of the time and timeless, attuned to current events and to eternity." Hayden's work was also informed by his Catholic faith, as he was a graduate student at both Xavier University in New Orleans and Notre Dame, two of America's premier Catholic institutions of higher learning.

> Other Hayden works of note are the Martin Luther King statue (dubbed "the egg") in New Orleans, and the Oliver Pollock statue in Baton Rouge.

The largest historically Black university in the world

Southern University in Baton Rouge is one of the largest historically Black universities in the world. Another Hayden work, *Lift Every Voice*, can be found on the university's campus as a tribute to two Southern students killed by police in a 1972 campus Black Panther protest – again, a timely and timeless subject in light of events following the 2020 death of Georg Floyd, which sparked many outpourings of civil unrest over issues that Hayden had immortalized with his artistic gift.

NEARBY

The serene park also has three beautiful tombs of Joseph S. Clark, Frances Clark, and Joseph Clark, sitting only feet away from *The Red Stick* on Scott's Bluff. The elder Clark was the president of Southern, and his son followed him in the post. Under the 47 years of Clark leadership, student numbers at Southern rose from 500 to 10,000.

MARTIN L. HARVEY HALL

Picasso and his cohorts borrowed from this body of work

Southern University Museum of Art, Scotlandville
225-771-4513 – suno.edu/page/susmuseums – viviankerr@subr.edu
Mon–Fri 10:30am–4:30pm

Martin L. Harvey Hall at Southern University's campus in Scotlandville, a suburb of Baton Rouge, is the home of an extraordinarily rich collection of African and African American art. From the outside it looks like a staid college building, but inside it shines as a depository of some of the richest and most influential styles.

Visitors see not only the art of Africa – which, with its angles, geometric patterns and stylized forms inspired the works of Picasso, Braque, Matisse and others in what became known in the early 20th century as modern abstraction and cubism – but also the work of African American artists such as New Orleans native JRenee Johnson, whose reverse glass painting style reflects her New Orleans roots. Her images are based on her experience in Hurricane Katrina, and shimmer with the vibrancy and exuberance of New Orleans culture.

Inside the eight galleries are major examples of Senufo, Dogon, Yoruba, Mende and other tribal styles, many from West Africa. The Bambara Chiwara, which became a go-to piece for catalogs and interior decoration, is here as well.

Among the artifacts on display are a series of cowrie-shell accessories, including a crown, ceremonial chairs, masks and headdresses that were often used in religious and important cultural rituals.

A bust of Barack Obama as you walk into the museum is poignant and meaningful when seen in such a setting.

The genesis of the museum (and of the two art museums at the other Southern campuses: see below) came from Dr. Leon Tarver II, the President of Southern from 1997 to 2005. Dr. Tarver was an avid art collector: His love of art, and his generosity in lending his collection to the museum here in Baton Rouge and in Shreveport, jump-started the museums into becoming a reality.

> Harvey Hall, which sits on the bank of the Mississippi, has a wonderful view of the river from the bluff.

Two other art museums

Founded in 1880, Southern University is the only Historically Black College and University (or "HBCU" as they are commonly referred to) in the United States that has a system of three campuses. Each campus now has an art museum whose mission is to preserve and present art, artifacts and other treasures of African American artists and artists of African descent.

SUMAS (Southern University Museum of Art), at the Shreveport campus, is tucked away in a modern complex, but its downtown location makes it the most accessible of the three museums. sumashreveport.org

SUNOMA (Southern University at New Orleans Museum of Art) is in the Art, Humanities and Social Studies building and was the last to be added. Visits by appointment only. suno.edu/page/SUNOMA

NORBERT RILLIEUX MODELS

The greatest invention in the history of American engineering?

West Baton Rouge Museum
845 North Jefferson Avenue, Port Allen, Baton Rouge
225-336-2422 – westbatonrougemuseum.com
Tue–Sat 10am–4:30pm, Sun 2pm–5pm

Inside the West Baton Rouge Museum, a working model of the multiple-effect evaporator stands as a tribute to one of the most significant American inventions, as well as to an inventor of whom you've probably never heard.

A free man of color, Norbert Rillieux was a French-speaking Creole (a person of mixed European and Black descent) born and raised in New Orleans, although even in his hometown most people today couldn't tell you anything about him. He was a chemical engineer and inventor educated at the École Centrale in Paris.

His invention was displayed at the Louisiana Purchase Exposition, also known as the St. Louis World's Fair (1904): It helped transform the sugar-refining business and exponentially enhanced its profitability.

The invention is well known in engineering circles and is generally recognized as the best method for lowering the temperature of all industrial evaporation, thereby saving large quantities of fuel. The process is used in any industry where large volumes of water must be evaporated,

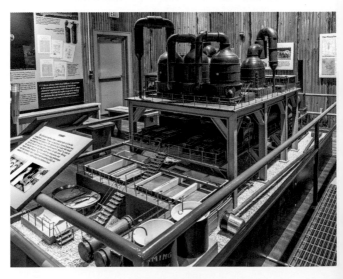

such as in water desalination.

Charles A. Browne, Jr., head of the U.S. Food and Drug Administration from 1924 to 1927, called the Rillieux process (which Rillieux patented in 1864) the greatest invention in the history of American engineering. Before Rillieux, the process of sugar refining had been slow, dangerous, expensive and inefficient.

As a Creole living in early 19th-century Louisiana, Rillieux enjoyed educational and social privileges not allowed or available to individuals of lower social status. He was the son of white plantation owner Vincent Rillieux and his *placée*, Constance Vivant, a free person of color. (A placée was a woman who joined a recognized civil union with a wealthy man and whose rights also applied to the children of that union.) This arrangement was prevalent in the French and Spanish colonies. In New Orleans, the offspring of these unions were often sent to be educated in France.

During the Yellow Fever epidemic that hit New Orleans in 1853, Rillieux devised a plan to combat the disease, but his scheme was thwarted by a former business associate who held a grudge against the Rillieux family.

Rillieux moved back to France in the late 1850s. Once in Europe, he developed a process to revolutionize the sugar beet industry, just as he had done with sugar cane in Louisiana.

A cousin of French painter Edgar Degas

A little-known fact: Rillieux was a first cousin-once-removed of the famous French painter Edgar Degas, whose aunt was Degas' grandmother.

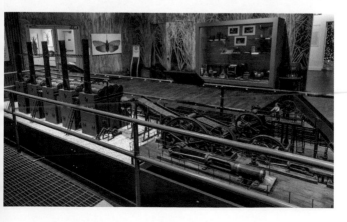

NATIONAL HANSEN'S DISEASE MUSEUM

Heart-wrenching tales about leprosy

5445 Point Clear Drive, Baton Rouge
225-642-1950
hrsa.gov.hansens-disease/museum
Tue–Sat 10am–4pm
The property is a National Guard base
IDs must be shown before entering the grounds

At a dead end along a Louisiana highway that traces the Mississippi River about 25 miles south of Baton Rouge, in what used to be a remote spot, you'll find a place that was once an entire world: The only hospital in the U.S. for people suffering from what used to be known as leprosy. Built in 1894, it is now the National Hansen's Disease Museum.

A star-shaped mosaic made out of Coca-Cola bottles sits right outside the museum: Its story hints at one of the unfortunate truths about this place.

The staff at Carville tried to give patients as "normal" a life as possible. There were dances, a bar, sports fields, a radio, a newspaper, and a cama-

raderie among the patients that lent a facade of normality, yet the outside world was always suspicious and fearful of lepers and nothing coming from them was allowed back into the 'normal world.' (Once you were a patient here, this was your home until the end. And it was also the end of the line for soft drink bottles.) This explains the repurposing of Coke bottles into a garden ornament.

Coca-Cola and other soft drink bottles were a universal presence in 20th-century America. But once the bottles had come into Carville, they couldn't be taken out again. So, with that joie de vivre that seems to spring from the human spirit even in the most challenging of times, the residents turned them into works of art.

The soft-drink-bottle art is just one of the heart-wrenching tales about even the simplest things in life that are found in this lovingly kept museum. The artifacts are not sanitized, like most modern tourist exhibits, but speak to our humanity in a quiet, dignified manner. It's a unique experience to see how this microworld functioned.

You are welcome to drive around the grounds and explore the buildings – all the patients were moved to other facilities long ago. But before visiting the museum, it's worth going into a small building adjacent to the parking lot that provides context, with a detailed timeline about the history of Carville.

Leprosy and the piggy bank

One of the more interesting things you'll run across in the museum is the piggy bank's connection with research into Hansen's Disease, a tale that has mostly been forgotten. Around 1906, a farm boy in Kansas called Wilbur Chapman received a gift of 3 silver dollars from a visitor named Mr. Danner. This Mr. Danner happened to be a missionary representing the American Leprosy Mission. Wilbur used the silver dollars to buy a pig, raised it, sold it for $25, and donated the money to the fight against leprosy. After some favorable press, the American Leprosy Mission used the story of Pete the Pig to inspire children worldwide to save money for leprosy in piggy banks. You'll find a few of these brass piggy banks on display in the museum.

The first patient was brought to Carville in the late 1880s, arriving by barge as most people wrongly believed that the disease was contagious.

A PENCIL-EMBEDDED CEILING

The result of a substantial bomb blast that rocked the Senate in 1970

Louisiana Senate Chamber
900 North Third Street, Baton Rouge
225-342-7317
crt.state.la.us/tourism/welcome-centers/state-capitol/
8am–4:30pm daily (except New Year's Day, Easter Sunday, Thanksgiving Day and Christmas Day)

As you enter the ornate Louisiana Senate Chamber after walking through the impressive mural entitled "The Abundance of Earth" from the Rotunda, look up as you enter the beautiful Art Deco Louisiana State Senate Chamber: You will see an object embedded in the ceiling in one of the 64 hexagonal tile sections, one for every parish in Louisiana. The object may be a little hard to glimpse from the vantage point of the Senate floor, but it's a pencil that has been stuck there since 1970. The best vantage point to see it is from the right side of the chamber.

The pencil, along with another piece of wood, came to be embedded at the top of one of the columns due to a substantial bomb blast that

rocked the Senate in 1970: Luckily, the chamber was empty as it was a Sunday morning. At a time when the Louisiana legislature was engaged in a heated debate on the passage of a right to work bill, many people believed the blast was related to this contentious labor issue.

There are press reports claiming that there was a note-taking responsibility for the bomb as retaliation for the police shooting of three African Americans. As time goes by, the truth seems to become more elusive. Whoever was responsible and whatever their motives, the culprits were never found.

Luckily the bomb, which was reported to be up to 30 sticks of dynamite, went off when there was no one in the chamber, and no one was hurt. However, the explosion was so powerful that it tore away the first few rows of the chamber; two of the original four marble columns had to be restored.

The Senate Chamber itself is a sight to behold, a masterpiece of Classicism and Art Deco. Built in 1939 to Huey Long's specifications amid the Great Depression, its lavish materials and artistic extravagance belie the fact that it was constructed in the midst of hard times. The ornate walls and columns of Famosa Violet marble from Germany and Brocatelle Violet marble from France speak to Long's goal to build a legacy. The floors are made from Roman travertine. The desks are fashioned from American walnut and inlaid with white holly. There are hand-carved chairs for every desk and Art Deco ornamentation wherever your eye wanders. Louisiana politics is often as colorful as the ornate Louisiana Capitol built by Huey Long. On September 8, 1935, Long was assassinated in the corridors of one of the crowning achievements of his political career. Whenever you find yourself in the Louisiana State Capitol, you should linger and take in the Art Deco majesty of the place. It's nothing short of a masterpiece of interior design.

ASSASSIN'S BULLET HOLES

The largest "tombstone" in the world

900 North Third Street,
Baton Rouge
225-342-7317
crt.state.las.us/tourism/welcome-center/state-capitol
Daily 8am–4:30pm

In the narrow hall outside the office of the President of the Louisiana Senate's office are what appear to be bullet holes. They are in the hall where Huey Long, a U.S. senator at the time, was mortally wounded by gunfire.

The holes are clearly visible and you may stick your finger or a ballpoint pen into one of them as generations of Louisianians have done for decades. The bullet-hole story is a staple of Capitol tours.

After years of differing versions of the shooting of Long, some researchers now claim that these are not bullet holes but only deterioration in the marble. The holes are there, and you can decide for yourself!

What is possibly true is that Long's death resulted from overzealous

bodyguards. On the night of September 8, 1936, Dr. Carl Weiss, who had a long-running family dispute with Long, confronted the senator in the hall. Shots soon rang out, and Weiss was shot dead by Long's bodyguards. Long was mortally wounded too, although most people did not realize at the time that his wounds would eventually kill him.

Many think that Long's bodyguards fired as many as 60 to 80 bullets: The ricochets were the culprit and caused the fatal wounds leading to Long's death.

Today, you may visit the crime scene in the beautiful pinkish marble hall where the shooting occurred. Behind a concrete pillar, across from the office of the Senate President, you'll see the most convincing bullet hole. There are other holes just down the marble hall, nearer to the office of the Speaker of the House.

Long was a national figure at the time of his death. Some believe that, with his populist message during the height of the Depression, he was the only man who could challenge President Franklin Roosevelt.

At the time of his death, Long was receiving some 60,000 letters a week. The Post Office in Washington, D.C. had two trucks to deliver mail, one for the senator's letters, the other for everyone else in the Congress.

Nonetheless, it is ironic that Long met his death in the impressive Louisiana Capitol he had built, an Art Deco masterpiece and the tallest State Capitol building in the U.S. He is buried in front of the Capitol, leading many people to muse that the building is the largest tombstone in the world.

GLASS DOME OF THE OLD LOUISIANA STATE CAPITOL

A magnificent harlequin-patterned glass dome

100 North Boulevard, Baton Rouge
224-342-7317
louisianaoldstatecapitol.org/visit
Mon–Fri 10am–4pm, Sat 9am–3pm

S itting on a bluff overlooking the Mississippi in the heart of Baton Rouge, the Old State Capitol appears to be a castle and is referred to by many as the "Castle of Baton Rouge."

The neo-Gothic, medieval-style building now has a new tan stucco exterior after renovations in the 1990s, but not even this unusual facade can prepare you for the unique interior.

Once inside the building, the focus moves to the center and the cast-iron spiral staircase that winds upward to a magnificent harlequin-patterned glass dome. This colorful feature was installed in 1882 by architect William A. Freret when he rebuilt the Capitol after it had been burned and gutted during the Civil War.

The building, which dates from 1847, was designed by architect James H. Dakin and was initially three stories. Legislators were always complaining that the building was too dark. Freret finally fixed that by adding a fourth floor and installing the spectacular glass dome.

Today, the building houses the Museum of Political History. It has many exhibits about Louisiana's governors, including an informative display covering Huey Long's political life and his death in 1935 (see p. 220).

The Capitol has had an eventful past as seat of the Louisiana legislature. In January 1861, it saw the secession vote to leave the Union. During the Civil War, it served as a prison as well as a barracks for African American troops. It also witnessed the impeachment trial of Huey Long before it was replaced in 1929–32 by the huge edifice that he built, and which now serves as the seat of Louisiana government.

As a piece of architecture, the "castle" invited ridicule from the outset. Local press reports called it an unsightly mass or a castle from the Dark Ages. In his book *Life on the Mississippi*, Mark Twain described it as an "architectural falsehood." He put the blame for its existence on Sir Walter Scott's novels, with their romantic notions of medieval knights and damsels.

The original architect, Dakin, defended his design, claiming that the plan was cost-effective and far removed from the Greco-Roman classical architectural style that was so over-used in America's public buildings.

Today, after the 1990s restoration, the riot of interior design is a triumph, with the salmon pink walls, green cast-iron fretwork, and gold highlights restored just as they appeared in Freret's day.

A 12-minute 4D immersive theatrical production called *The Ghost in the Capitol* chronicles the history of this remarkable building.

THE GUN AND BULLETS LINKED TO THE ASSASSINATION OF HUEY LONG

Missing for almost 50 years

Louisiana Old State Capitol, Baton Rouge
100 North Boulevard
225-342-0500
louisianaoldstatecapitol.org
Mon–Fri 10:30am–2:30pm

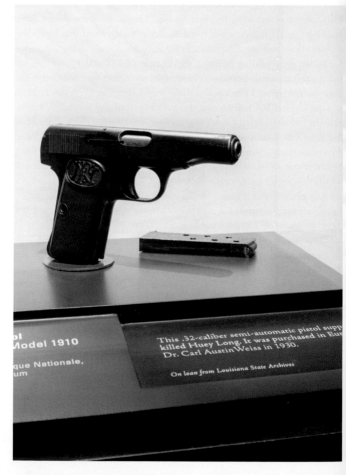

Tucked away in a dramatically lit room in the Louisiana Old State Capitol are a gun and two bullets linked to the assassination of Senator Huey Long in September 1935. An FN Model 1910, the gun owned by Dr. Carl Weiss, the accused assassin, sits in a glass case at a poised angle on red fabric.

After it had been missing for almost 50 years, the gun was found and reclaimed by the Weiss family and donated to the Louisiana State Police.

The bullets found with the gun were on the property of Louis Guerre, who at the time of Long's death was head of the Louisiana Criminal Bureau of Investigation.

Although no ballistic or medical evidence was presented at the inquest into Long's death, the official story is that Weiss shot Long in the chest and was subsequently killed by Long's bodyguards, known as the Cossacks or Skullcrushers. However, many reports claim that Weiss did not shoot Long but instead punched him in the face and that it was the bodyguards who opened fire on Weiss. Weiss was said to have been shot over 60 times. An exhumation of his body many years later found that he had been hit at least 24 times.

Since Long held a life insurance policy, the report by K. B. Ponder, who investigated the senator's death for the MONY Life Insurance Company in 1935, sheds a fascinating light on what may have been the cause of death. Ponder's report, which was only made available to the public in 1985, reads as follows: "There is no doubt that Weiss attacked Long, but there is considerable doubt that Weiss ever fired a gun." The report continues: "There is no doubt that [Long's] death was accidental, but the consensus of more informed opinion is that he was killed by his own guard and not by Weiss."

A ballistic test by the Smithsonian Institution in 1991 showed that the bullet did not come from Weiss's gun, lending credence to the belief held by many that Dr. Weiss did not shoot Long.

HIDDEN SYMBOLS
OF THE OZOLS MURAL

Secret messages for each governor

Louisiana Governor's Mansion
1001 Capitol Access Road, Baton Rouge
225-342-5855
governorsmansion.org
Tours by appointment

Visible by appointment only (see website), the Louisiana Governor's Mansion boasts a beautiful mural depicting some of the state's charms and signature symbols such as a pelican, a crawfish and the abundant coastal waters. Although the existence of the mansion is not a secret, the painting has numerous hidden messages for each governor who has resided at the house, a trademark of New Orleans-based artist Auseklis Ozols, who received the commission to paint the mural during the administration of Mike Foster (1996–2004). It's fun to try and find them and link them to each governor.

In the Grand Isle scene, Governor Murphy "Mike" Foster III and his bride, Alice Foster, walk hand in hand on the beach. Foster's hunting camp features a sign that says "1492–1892", as 1892 was the year that his grandfather, Murphy J. Foster, was elected governor of Louisiana.

The elephant in a pirogue is a reference to Dave Treen (1980–84), the first Republican governor of Louisiana since Reconstruction.

In a corner, a deck of playing cards is an acknowledgment of Edwin Edwards' (1992–96) reputation for gambling: It was widely known that Edwards held regular poker games in the governor's mansion during his administration.

A rainbow is for Governor Kathleen Blanco (2004–08) and the diversity brought to the office by Louisiana's first woman governor.

The guitar near a sunflower is for country singing star Jimmie Davis, who went on to become governor from 1960 to 1964. His signature song, "You Are My Sunshine," was a Gold Record hit.

Other "hidden" objects are a cardinal, a mouse, a baseball bat, a ladybug, three eggs in a nest, a chicken in a pot, a camouflage hat, Mardi Gras beads and a turtle (a symbol of how long it took to approve and build the Superdome in New Orleans).

In one corner there are hurricane warning flags, an acknowledgment of another Louisiana reality: They were placed there in 2005 after Hurricanes Rita and Katrina had devastated much of southern Louisiana.

In 2023 Ozols was back at the mansion to honor the outgoing governor John Bel Edwards (2016– 24) with his first rifle and his airborne ranger beret. There is also an old-fashioned doctor bag in recognition of Edwards' expansion of Medicaid in Louisiana and (in a nod to one of the other defining issues of Edwards' time in office) a vaccination syringe and Covid masks.

OLIVER POLLOCK STATUE

The leading financial contributor to the American Revolution

238 North Boulevard #200
Downtown Baton Rouge

A highly stylized public statue in the heart of downtown Baton Rouge depicts one of the greatest unsung heroes of the American Revolution. Indeed, Oliver Pollock is all but unknown to generations of Americans, yet his importance in American history is unquestionable.

The sculpture is the work of noted artist Frank Hayden, known for his many public sculptures in Louisiana, including one of Martin Luther

King Jr. in New Orleans. The downtown Baton Rouge piece is the only statue of Pollock known to exist.

Oliver Pollock was an Irishman who made his fortune in the Caribbean in pre-revolutionary times and was a citizen of New Orleans when the American Revolution broke out. He was named official representative of the Colonies in New Orleans (at the time, Spanish territory) by the Continental Congress.

In this role he raised money from third parties on behalf of the war effort, eventually contributing more funds to it than even France, Spain and the Dutch banks. His contributions, unlike those of heralded figures such as George Washington, Paul Revere, Benjamin Franklin and Alexander Hamilton, did not make it into many history texts, and so he remains unknown to most Americans.

Pollock's financial and organizational acumen was instrumental in the successful prosecution of the war: He raised troops and purchased supplies for the Spanish governor of Louisiana, Bernardo de Gálvez, whose army went on to defeat the British forces in Florida, Alabama, Mississippi and Louisiana, never losing a single engagement. Historians believe that this victorious military campaign by Gálvez, as well as that of George Rogers Clark in the Midwest, would not have been possible without Pollock's efforts and financial contributions. For his support, Pollock was given the nickname "Financier of the Revolution in the West."

The plaza that holds his statue features an elaborate frieze depicting the soldiers and citizens who participated in the Battle of Baton Rouge, the only Revolutionary War battle fought in Louisiana. That early victory for Governor Gálvez cleared the Lower Mississippi Valley of the British military presence.

The origin of the dollar sign

Pollock's other claim to fame (had he ever known any!), and the one that may be his most enduring contribution to history, derives from his financial dealings. Since his fortune had been made in the Spanish colonies, including Louisiana, his monetary transactions were handled using the Spanish *peso*, a globally circulated silver coin generally referred to by North American English speakers as a "dollar;" his shorthand version of "peso" in his ledgers was a melding of the letters p and s into one symbol. When this symbol was adopted by his friend and U.S. Superintendent of Finance, Founding Father Robert Morris, to designate the new currency of the United States of America, the dollar sign was born.

SING THE RIVER SCULPTURE

When the river sings

Florida Street and North River Road, Baton Rouge

On the levee at the Mississippi River, *Sing the River* is a shiny, futuristic, stainless-steel sculpture by California-based artist, Po Shu Wang. It was funded by a grant from the Baton Rouge Rotary Club to celebrate its 100th birthday and installed in 2019.

Unlike most sculptures, this 14-ft.-high spherical design is equipped with special technology that allows it to convert the movement, height and flow of the Mississippi River into what sounds just like singing. This is done by means of sensors in the river connected to the sculpture.

Visitors can listen to the singing and communicate with it. You can actually talk back by speaking or by pressing a button that takes the input of human activity and then changes the way the sensors respond to the different frequencies from both the river and the visitor.

The sculpture is an example of bioarchitecture, described as "the design and construction of buildings in an ecologically friendly manner." The idea is to look to nature for inspiration and innovation.

Here, on the Mississippi, *Sing the River* is a smaller and simpler interpretation of nature's forms. The reflective surface allows for a unique photo op – you can take a photo of your own reflection and the image often results in a kind of funhouse distortion.

Bioarchitecture

Other well-known bioarchitecture structures include Anish Kapoor's Cloud Gate ("the Bean") in Chicago, Gaudí's Sagrada Família in Barcelona, the "Bird's Nest" Olympic stadium in Beijing, and Santiago Calatrava's "Turning Torso" apartment building in Malmö, Sweden (modeled after the natural movements of the human torso). A more accessible comparison might be Frank Lloyd Wright's "organic architecture" at Fallingwater, where the structure is transparently intertwined with nature.

HUEY LONG'S SECRET STAIRWAY ⑲

An escape from unwanted visitors

Old Governor's Mansion
502 North Boulevard, Baton Rouge
225-342-9778
laogm.org
Mon–Fri 9am–4pm

On the first floor of the Old Governor's Mansion, a nondescript wooden door leads to a wooden staircase up to the office of Huey Long, the first governor to live here. If you open the door, you'll be greeted by a shadowy, life-sized wooden cut-out of Long in a white linen suit with a white hat on his head. This was the secret stairway that the governor had built so he could escape unwanted visitors.

Long built the Old Governor's Mansion after he had torn down the old governor's residence, using prison labor in defiance of the wishes of the Louisiana State Legislature.

Today's visitor may be struck by the building's grandeur. Don't miss the beautiful winding staircase that brings you up to the governor's bedroom. This is the staircase that Huey avoided with his secret stairway. The bedroom is still as it would have been in Long's day, with his office next door.

On the desk in the upstairs office, you'll see a copy of the sheet music and a record of "Every Man a King," a song Long co-wrote for the campaign trail. Long was a well-known political figure nationally and dreamed of being elected president of the United States. His books, *Share Our Wealth* and *My First Days in the White House*, are also here on the desk.

Visiting the mansion is a pleasant way to spend a few hours as there are touches of the other governors who lived here, but Long's influence is all over the place.

The bathrooms have no bathtubs, only showers, because Long believed that important, busy men did not have time to take baths.

The mansion was refurbished to its current state between 1996 and 1998 and reopened as a tourist destination the following year.

One interesting feature of the mansion is the nice display of Governor Jimmie Davis's career as a singing cowboy, with saddles, movie memorabilia, guitars, and his gold record for "You Are My Sunshine."

The building is now a sought-after destination for wedding receptions.

Built to mimic the White House

Legend has it that Huey Long had the mansion built to mimic the White House as he intended to occupy it in the not-too-distant future! It was built from the architectural plans of Thomas Jefferson.

DINING ROOM WALLPAPER AT THE OLD GOVERNOR'S MANSION

Idyllic scenes of an emerging America

Old Governor's Mansion
502 North Boulevard, Baton Rouge
225-387-2464 – oldgovernorsmansion.com
Mon–Fri 9am–4pm

In the dining room at the Old Governor's Mansion, the glamorous mansion built by Huey Long, it is easy not to notice the beautiful 19th-century wallpaper. Designed in France by Jean-Julian Deltil in 1834 for Zuber and Co. of Alsace (in a pattern known as "Scenic America" and still available from the company today), this particular wallpaper design can be found in only four places in the country: here at the Governor's Mansion, at Brown University, in Natchez, and at the White House, where it was installed at the behest of First Lady Jaqueline Kennedy in 1961 during a celebrated refurbishing of the White House.

Curiously, Deltil had never visited America, so the scenes he created (New York City as seen from New Jersey, West Point on the Hudson, a view of Boston, a natural bridge in Virginia, and Niagara Falls, among

others) are based on an idyllic vision of America. One important thing to notice is that the African Americans are portrayed as equals to the white Americans, in both dress and social standing. This provides a fascinating insight into how Europeans saw life in America at that time.

The beautiful wallpaper was renovated in 2022 by Elise Grenier, an art restorer from Louisiana, who has also worked on some of the state's most treasured artworks, including the murals at the State Capitol and at LSU's Allen Hall.

The wallpaper was printed using 1,674 woodblocks, with a separate carving for each color representation. The sky (light blue to dark blue) was hand-painted before the scenes were added.

ART HOUSE ㉑

A one-of-a-kind artwork, so you can explore your inner child

2598 Dalrymple Drive, Baton Rouge
Private residence

On the corner of Dalrymple Drive and April Street, fronting City Park Lake near LSU in Baton Rouge, the house at 2598 Dalrymple Drive jumps out as quite a surprise in this somewhat high-end neighborhood. It's the work and vision of Dr. Joel Podolsky.

The modern sculpture outside the house is a one-of-a-kind work in several parts but the metal sculpture that fronts April Street is the most accessible part of the ensemble.

The materials are all old car parts, notably mufflers and muffler pipes painted and arranged to great and joyful effect, together with other remnants of found metal fashioned into flowers, musical notes and other items in fantastic shapes. The impact of the found objects often inspires passersby to leave stuff for Dr. Podolsky to reuse in his artistic endeavor.

The front-yard creations are more difficult to see as you drive by as they're partially hidden by foliage, but if you stop you can get a nice view.

Walking around the property, you'll find new things at every viewing. The total effect is the very definition of whimsy.

Dr. Podolsky stretched working on the multifaceted artwork in 1993 after the death of his parents as a form of therapy and looks upon the work as a labor of love inspired by the story of Jack and the Beanstalk.

A continual work-in-progress, the owner sees his house as a quest for a second chance at childhood. He also hopes that the house will inspire others to explore their inner child.

Dr. Podolsky calls his work "artscaping" as opposed to landscaping.

AUDUBON DAY

Once a year, the public is invited to view a masterpiece

Hill Memorial Library at LSU
225-578-2054
lib.lsu.edu
Access only one day a year
Online registration is required, and access is limited to 40 people for an hour each
A different date is chosen each year, so check ahead on the library's website

Once a year, on Audubon Day, on the second floor of the Hill Memorial Library at LSU, the public is invited to get a rare up-close and personal look at John James Audubon's masterpiece, The Birds of America, one of the most famous publishing feats in history. It was a worldwide sensation in its day and remains so.

These well-known images of America's birds are found in the permanent collection of the Hill Memorial Library at LSU in an original subscription 'double-elephant' folio edition. The elephant folios are so called because of their size (the pages measure 28.5 x 3.5 in.): They are so large that two people are required to carry them.

The viewing is held on the second floor of the library's McIlhenny Room. Laid out on wooden tables, the pages of Volumes 1–4 are turned simultaneously by museum personnel.

Audubon was told that he must be crazy to print such a large book, but after much effort, and promotion by subscription in both America and England, the printing was an unprecedented success. Only 120 of the original copies are known to exist.

Audubon is closely related to Louisiana as he painted and researched his work (or completed 23 of his paintings) while in the state, where he served as a tutor at Oakley Plantation in nearby St. Francisville. In fact, 'Wild Turkey' was executed at Oakley and is the most famous and valuable of his bird paintings.

The work consists of 435 hand-colored, life-size prints made from engraved plates. The images include five or six birds that are believed to be extinct. Two of the original subscribers were American statesmen Daniel Webster and Henry Clay.

The double-elephant folio edition was purchased by LSU in 1964 from the Duke of Northumberland and was one of the original subscription copies. It was financed by a grant from the Crown Zellerbach Foundation and restored with funds from the Coypu Foundation. The purchase price was an estimated $64,000, and today the folio is believed to be worth around $10 million.

Audubon Day at the Hill Memorial Library also involves representatives of the LSU Museum of Natural History, who bring photographs, reference materials and other significant bird-related books for the public to see.

During Audubon Day, veterinary students from the LSU Veterinary School bring live birds from the Resident Raptors program and offer behind-the-scenes tours of the LSU Museum of Natural Science's extensive bird collection.

The original Mike the Tiger is not the one you think …

Natural History Museum
119 Foster Hall, LSU, Baton Rouge
225-578-2855
lsu.edu
Mon–Fri 8am–4pm

Many of the visitors who come to football, baseball, or basketball games at LSU every year also make a pilgrimage to see the LSU mascot, Mike the Tiger, a living, breathing, prowling Bengal tiger, just outside the east end of Tiger Stadium. However, most do not know that the original Mike the Tiger is not far away and available for viewing.

In the heart of the maze of buildings that make up the core of the LSU campus, the Natural History Museum at Foster Hall is a Smithsonian type of natural history museum in miniature: The displays are in a very tight space but you could spend hours taking it all in.

Mike the First died in 1956 at the age of twenty, a much longer life than most tigers, but the search to replace him was not so easy. As the hunt dragged on, officials decided that a stuffed mascot was better than none, so he was taxidermized and here he stands today.

His glass case has a panel to the right with five white buttons that conjure up the various sounds a tiger makes, with an explanation of what each sound means. One, of course, is the roar that Mike used to make on football Saturday nights.

The rest of the exhibits are beautifully executed: There are dioramas of North American wildlife such as the bear and moose and a diorama set in Cameron Parish that displays over 60 geese and ducks. Southern Louisiana in the winter boasts the largest concentration of waterfowl in North America (also on display here).

The Lowery Hall of Birds features many of the 432 bird species who live in Louisiana for at least part of their lives, including a Passenger Pigeon (extinct), an Ivory-billed Woodpecker (extinct), and a Brown Pelican (endangered but coming back, due to human intervention). At the end of the hall, a door to the left simply saying "Collection" opens onto a warehouse housing one of the most renowned collections of birds and mammals in the world and is available to researchers from around the world.

Once upon a time, Mike was even rolled out in a cage, accompanied by LSU cheerleaders who would entice him to roar, to the delight of the sellout crowds at Tiger Stadium.

ALLEN HALL MURALS

Outstanding examples of mural artwork

LSU Campus, Baton Rouge
225-578-8863

A colorful and sometimes controversial series of frescoes adorns the hallways and stairwell of Allen Hall in the heart of the LSU campus. The robust figures, portrayed in a style popular in the 1930s and reminiscent of Works Progress Administration (WPA) artwork of the time, were not produced with WPA funds but were funded entirely by LSU.

These outstanding examples of mural artwork were executed by five LSU art students under the direction of LSU art professor Conrad Albrizio, an internationally known fresco painter who was also the first professor of painting at LSU. Albrizio's other works of note include paintings at the Louisiana Capitol building and at the Union Passenger Terminal in New Orleans. Painted in 1954, they show a decided Cubist bent in his style by the 1950s.

Each student had leeway as to the content of the paintings. This led to a bit of political posturing, and some of the paintings installed during the 1940s and World War II had political overtones, including images of Hitler and Mussolini that were later removed by LSU administrators.

The remaining murals depict scenes from agriculture and science, other endeavors tagged to the Louisiana economy, and are emblematic of LSU's contribution as a center of education in these fields.

In the 1960s some of the murals were covered over by white paint while others were buried by the addition of a stairwell.

In 2001 Elise Grenier, an LSU graduate and renowned art restorer, who had been working professionally in Italy for 25 years, was commissioned to restore the remaining murals. It was a meticulous job because they were analyzed with a non-invasive chemical, and dry cleaning was followed by a deionized water applied to Japanese rice paper to remove the accumulated dust. Others were chosen for restoration because of environmental issues such as water damage over the four decades during which the murals had been covered up.

The scenes include anglers, agricultural workers, oil workers, scientists, and aviators, all designed to portray Louisiana as it was in the 1930s.

In recent times, complaints have surfaced about the depiction of African Americans and plans are under consideration to paint new murals on the other side of the hallways at Allen Hall to respect more modern sensibilities.

These beautiful murals – once almost lost or concealed by paint and obscured by architectural remodeling – are now here for the world to enjoy.

WILLIAM A. BROOKSHIRE
LSU MILITARY MUSEUM

Celebrating LSU's many military contributions

92 Tower Drive, Baton Rouge
225-334-2003
lsu.edu/brookshire-museum/index.php
Mon–Fri 10am–3pm

Hidden under the LSU Memorial Tower (1926), which remembers all Louisiana citizens who died in World War I, the William A. Brookshire LSU Military Museum is a crisp and polished museum dedicated to LSU students and faculty who served in the U.S. military from the Civil War to recent action in the Middle East.

From its beginning, LSU has had a military connection. The fact that Union general William Tecumseh Sherman was its first president may seem a strange irony as, soon after taking the reins of the newly minted university, Sherman resigned to fight for the Union and against the students, most of whom joined the Confederate cause.

The museum has numerous artifacts and texts explaining the vital and frequently under-reported contributions to the U.S. military of brave ex-students, both women and men. Here are a few:

After representing LSU on the gridiron in the 1944 Orange Bowl, Joe Nagata joined the U.S. Army and eventually won a Bronze Star while serving with the 442nd Regimental Combat Team, consisting almost exclusively of second-generation Japanese Americans. The 442nd unit is the most highly decorated unit in the history of the U.S. military. It has been awarded 9,486 Purple Hearts and 21 Congressional Medals of Honor.

Female trailblazers are also represented, such as Brigadier General Karlynn Peltz O'Shaughnessy, who won a Bronze Star for service in the Gulf Wars; Lieutenant General Terry Gabreski, who served as mentor to the first class of female cadets at the U.S. Air Force Academy in 1980; and 1996 LSU graduate Major Meredith Brown, who fought in Iraq as a U.S. Marine in 2008.

A stadium named after a baseball player killed in action

LSU's baseball stadium, Alex Box Stadium, is named in honor of Simeon A. Box, a star athlete and baseball player at LSU who was killed in action while preparing to take part in the battle at Kasserine Pass in Tunisia (1943). He is buried in Carthage, Tunisia.

BRONZE PLAQUE AT GATE 10

A forgotten memory of the legendary Tiger Stadium dorms

Section 10 Tiger Stadium
Nicholson and North Stadium Road, Baton Rouge
lsusports.net/facilities/tiger-stadium

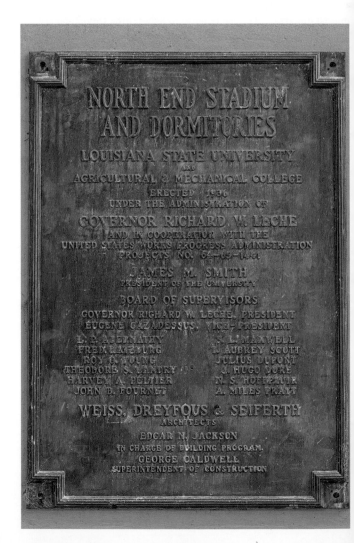

Next to the entrance at Gate 10, a neglected bronze plaque commemorates the legendary LSU stadium dormitories which have housed literally tens of thousands of students since the 1930s. The spartan conditions inside the unusually situated dorms have become legendary.

Today the remaining dorm rooms are empty but there were once as many as 1,500 students living there. But why were there dormitories in a stadium?

Huey Long (1893–1935), the legendary Louisiana governor, wanted to build a bigger stadium than the original Tiger Stadium, which had a seating capacity of 12,000 (today, the official capacity stands at 102,321), but the legislature would not agree.

Enter Thomas "Skipper" Heard, the new director of LSU athletics. Heard knew that the Louisiana legislature had approved over $250,000 for the building of dormitories at LSU. He either quipped or seriously believed that the money could be used to build dorms attached to the stadium and expand the stadium capacity on top of the dorms. Long got wind of the idea, and that is just what he did.

One of the unexpected consequences of the expansion on top of the dorms was that the architects had to make the rake of the seating area significantly steeper than otherwise necessary to accommodate the dorms. This bowl (and the decibels it helped to create) has served LSU football well as it is known throughout college football as one of the loudest venues in the land! In 2007, ESPN called Tiger Stadium "the scariest place to play" and "by far the loudest stadium in the country."

> ## "As long as I don't smell it or hear it, I don't care"
> One residential assistant (as the dorm supervisors were known) was said to have remarked about enforcing discipline among the students: "As long as I don't smell it or hear it, I don't care."

Two of LSU's most heralded football players, Y. A. Tittle and Steve Van Buren – both elected to the Pro Football Hall of Fame – were once residents of these dorms.

LSU LINEUP BLACKBOARD

A remembrance of times gone by that most fans will never see

LSU Facility Service Building, Baton Rouge – Engineering Lane
225-578-3186
faciltyservices@lsu.edu

On a wall in the maintenance barn at LSU, you'll see a relic from days ago that would still resonate with die-hard LSU fans … if they only knew it was there. The board shows the results of a football game with SEC opponent Vanderbilt in 1946, with the final score of LSU 14 and Vanderbilt 0.

It's a chalkboard with the starting lineup of the 1946 Bayou Bengals, a team that lost only one game in 1946 and that upset Alabama and the future Number One pick of the National Football League (NFL) draft in 1947, Harry Gilmer.

The 1946 LSU Tigers ended up sixth in the AP poll. This team was said by long-time LSU broadcaster and voice of the Tigers John Ferguson to be the best LSU team he ever saw … and that included its first national champion team in 1958.

If you read the names on the board, you'll see several players who went on to play in the NFL. Y. A. Titte, who died in 2016 at the age of 93, is arguably the most famous player in LSU football history … at least until Joe Burrow came along in 2019 to lead LSU to the National Championship.

Yelberton Abraham Tittle Jr., known as Y.A., was notable for his name, which was somewhat unusual, and for the photo of him on his knees without his helmet, a stream of blood running down from his head, taken in the New York Giants' losing effort in the 1963 NFL championship game. This is one of the most iconic pictures in NFL history and is recognized even by casual fans. Tittle went on to be inducted into the Pro Football Hall of Fame, so when you see a blackboard with Y. A. Tittle chalked in, this immediately grabs the attention of LSU fans.

That day, others in the lineup were Ray Coates, who played for the New York Giants and became a notable high-school coach at Jesuit in New Orleans, and Jim Cason, who played for the San Francisco 49ers. Ed Champagne played with the LA Rams and, notably, with Paul "Tank" Younger on the Rams. Younger was the first player from Grambling University (an HBCU), to play in the NFL; in those days, if a Black and a white player from Louisiana wanted to play on the same team, they had to go pro.

LSU CAMPUS MOUNDS

The oldest human-fabricated structures in the Americas

133 North Stadium Road, Baton Rouge
lsu.edu/mounds/index.php

In the heart of the LSU campus, two 20-ft. mounds, known for years on campus as simply the "Indian mounds", have recently been discovered by LSU geologists to be the oldest human-fabricated structures in the Americas.

Estimated to be 11,300 years old, these mounds might be not only the oldest remaining structures in the Western Hemisphere, but on Earth. They would predate the Pyramids of Egypt and Stonehenge by thousands of years and also predate the structures at Göbekli Tepe in Turkey.

Dr. Brooks Elwood's carbon dating of ash taken from the site at LSU, which has Tiger Stadium as a close backdrop, backs up his claims about the age of these ceremonial structures. He surmises that the temperatures resulting from the burning of reed and cane, as well as mammal bones, were too hot for cooking. Therefore, they are thought to be

the site of religious ceremonies that may have even included the burning of humans.

The first mound, Mound B, is the oldest. Geologists estimate that Mound A was built some 7,500 years ago. After thousands of years, both achieved their present-day height of 20 ft.

Astronomers at LSU have found that the tops of both mounds are aligned at 8.5 degrees, which would point to the eastern night sky with the red giant star Arcturus, one of the brightest stars that can be seen from Earth.

Today, even though the mounds are deemed to be of such great historical importance, there is only a flimsy chain-link fence surrounding them.

Recently, a historical sign was erected after a Native American student organization complained to the university authorities about an unfortunate incident of students using the mounds for recreation: In 2001 an ice storm canceled classes, and a local TV reporter shot a video of students sledding down the ancient mounds on baking sheets, plastic boxes and a kayak.

With Tiger Stadium so close, the mounds have sometimes been used as tailgating venues, and in the past sometimes even had automobiles driving over them.

LSU DESIGN SCULPTURE GARDEN

"The thought-provoking nature of artistic expression"

College of Art and Design
102 Design Building
Between Atkinson Hall and Art Studio building,
LSU campus, Baton Rouge
225-578-5400
design.lsu.edu

Hidden in a small quad among the maze of buildings on the LSU campus, you may stumble upon a quiet, curious space strewn with modern sculptures born out of the imagination of students at the LSU College of Art and Design. In this outdoor space, you can contemplate the world while surrounded by, among other things, a tall blue metallic chair suitable for an unknown sitter.

The quad that sits between Atkinson Hall and the Art Studio building can be a revelation when first encountered. Students use it as a secret spot to meet friends and unwind from the bustle of campus or studies. Under the majestic magnolia trees and oaks, surrounded by various artistic visions, you will also find a pair of swings.

At first, confusion might set in. Although we're used to seeing public art in urban spaces, we are often unsure whether a free-standing object is an artwork or not. But here the objects are just … swings. Here, students can avail themselves of the child-like feel of defying gravity, if only for a moment. Among the art displayed here, the swing experience seems to fit with the whimsy of the sculptures (both permanent and temporary) created by LSU students.

The college's official website shows the sculpture area as an integral part of the school: It sometimes blends disciplinary investigations and collaborative ventures. LSU has an extensive sculpture program, and its goals of developing an individual aesthetic or vision in both traditional and non-traditional styles make the sky the limit. This type of creativity requires the best facilities and LSU has some of the finest artistic tools on any U.S. campus. These include a complete woodworking shop, fully equipped welding and fabricating facilities, a forging station and a foundry for working bronze, aluminum, and iron.

LSU art students' and faculty work can also be found at the Shaw Center for the Arts on the 5th floor, and in the Alfred C. Glassell Exhibition Gallery and the Union Gallery at the LSU Student Union. There is also a pop-up locker gallery in the hallway of the Studio Arts building. Or you might just want to linger in the quad and swing a bit …

ALLOSAURUS SKELETON

A full-size dinosaur hidden in the heart of Baton Rouge

Howe-Russell Kniffen Geoscience Complex (Room E235)
LSU (Louisiana State University), Baton Rouge
225-578-3353
geology@lsu.edu
lsu.edu/science/geology/contact_us/index.php

For those in search of something to assuage the curiosity and almost lustful desire for dinosaurs of the younger members of the family, love this: a convenient full-size dinosaur hidden in the heart of Baton Rouge that is easily accessible to the public.

Inside LSU, the focal point in a three-story atrium just inside the main entrance of the new building in the Howe-Russell Kniffen Geo-Science Complex is indeed a full-size skeleton of an Allosaurus. The dinosaur poses in what could be described as a trot – a cool surprise for most people who happen upon it on the first floor of the building.

During daylight hours, the atrium is lit by a large skylight, which keeps the room quite warm, presumably a temperature that might make an Allosaurus feel at home.

The high ceiling with its huge aluminum fan hanging from the ceiling, and the wooden tables furnishing the room, make this a quiet, welcoming space to study. There are usually a few students working away on their laptops and scattered around the Allosaurus in its triangular corner display.

What is an Allosaurus?

Allosaurus means "different lizard" in Greek; it gets its name from its unique concave vertebrae. It was a large bipedal predator that preyed on plant eaters and carnivores alike and, it is believed, on its own kind. With a skull equipped with dozens of serrated teeth and a length of over 28 ft., heavily muscled hind limbs and smaller three-fingered sharpened claws and a large, long muscled tail for balance, the Allosaurus was at the top of the food chain during its heyday some 145 to 155 million years ago.

Other ancient artifacts to whet the dinosaur appetite

If you're in an adventurous mood, there are other nearby ancient artifacts to whet the dinosaur appetite. The old wing of the GeoScience Complex has dinosaur tracks that were found in Louisiana and, in the same room as the fossil tracks, you'll see an impressive mammoth tusk and mammoth dental work.

Earthquake-like numbers

The GeoScience Complex itself has a unique link to LSU and Tiger Stadium that goes through its seismograph. Two notable events at the nearby stadium have registered earthquake-like numbers. On October 8, 1988, after a Tommy Hodson touchdown pass to Eddie Fuller in the waning moments of the 4th quarter in the Auburn game, the crowd reaction was registered as a legitimate earthquake on the seismograph in the Louisiana Geological Survey office on campus. And in April 2022, a Garth Brooks concert did the same trick.

TEXTILE AND COSTUME MUSEUM

A one-of-a-kind showcase

140 Human Ecology Building, LSU, Baton Rouge
225-578-5992
textilemuseum.huec.lsu.edu
Mon–Fri 9am–4:30pm

S ituated in the Human Ecology Building on the LSU campus, the Textile and Costume Museum packs an incredible punch with changing exhibits that feature the extensive collection of over 15,000 pieces held by the LSU Department of Textiles, Apparel Design and Merchandising.

The purpose of the exhibition space, inaugurated in 1992 thanks to donations, is to promote conservation, research, teaching and public service and to showcase the history of textiles, clothing, costumes and fabric over the years.

Started in the 1930s as a teaching collection, it runs the gamut of apparel, accessories, ethnic and household textiles, piece goods, books, clothing patterns and more. It has a global reach and even has garments going back to prehistoric times.

The museum often showcases the crucial role played by women in American history. The exhibit "Dream Stitches" (dedicated to a baby's layettes and first clothes) is a case in point. One of the curious facts revealed by this exhibit was that in the U.S. in 1914, pink was considered the color of baby boys and blue the color of girls.

Other exhibits have included "Quilts of the Cane River Plantation," which highlights the importance of quilts in Louisiana culture; a beautiful survey of colorful Guatemalan regional designs; and "Converting Commodity Bags: Recycling Circa 1940."

The commodity bag exhibit is an example of the fascinating history and stories that can be woven from everyday fabrics. These bags were usually hand woven at home and were used to carry grain to and from the mill. Firms soon started to manufacture these bags, and by the end of the 19th century, they were the preferred packaging of a growing mercantile economy. Even catalogs such as Montgomery Ward started to sell empty commodity bags as they were sought-after and put to many uses. A 100-lb. chicken feed sack would provide 1 yard of fabric for a woman's apron and a small tablecloth would make a set of kitchen curtains. Three or more of these sacks could be turned into a woman's dress.

This exhibit also included booklets made by high school students in home economics classes in the 1920s that explained how to transform these commodity bags into fashion and other utilitarian objects. The Great Depression and the shortages during World War II also gave an impetus to the practice and use of the bags.

LSU RURAL LIFE MUSEUM

A tranquil oasis of nature, beauty and history

4560 Essen Lane, Baton Rouge
225-765-2437 – lsuagcenter.com/portals/burden
Open 7 days a week
Rural Life Museum and Windrush Gardens: 8am–5pm
Visitor Center and historic structures: 8am–4:30pm
Admission fee

The LSU Rural Life Museum sits concealed amidst the ever-burgeoning urban sprawl of Baton Rouge as a tranquil oasis of nature, beauty and history. Once you turn off of the highway onto the property of the Burden Museum and Gardens, you will travel just a few hundred yards through farmland maintained by the museum before being transported back into the 19th century.

The Rural Life Museum is part of the Burden Museum complex that sits on the former Windrush Plantation, founded in the early 1800s. The land was donated in 1966 by the surviving siblings and sister-in-law of William Pike Burden Jr. to preserve and create a place for research into the rural culture and legacy of Louisiana agricultural communities.

The surviving buildings include pioneer cabins, a country church, Acadian House and a dogtrot house that reveal the variety of styles and ethnic diversity that formed the rural culture of Louisiana.

The plantation structures are furnished with authentic artifacts and showcase the lives of the enslaved people who lived there.

The Exhibit Barn boasts literally thousands of items from 19th-century as well as early 20th-century farm life. Other authentic plantation structures include a commissary, a kitchen, slave cabins, a sugar mill, a schoolhouse and a blacksmith shop.

Some of the old buildings are masterpieces of eroded simplicity that reveal how simple and primitive things were not so long ago.

The Burden campus is a key location for undergraduate and graduate students of LSU AgCenter as it gives a hands-on insight into the origins of the local agricultural society. The Burden Gardens are maintained by LSU, are free to the public and include a tranquil 3-mile walking trail.

The Burden Museum campus also includes an array of attractions that can make this an all-day excursion for the visitor: 440 acres in all, including a rose garden, an herb garden, a pollinator garden, an arboretum, six birding loops, many walking trails, a children's playground and, of course, the splendid old buildings.

One of the top ten outdoor museums in the world

In the 1980s, the British Museum named the LSU Rural Life Museum – which boasts over 30 authentically preserved buildings amidst its farmland – one of the top ten outdoor museums in the world.

LSU HILLTOP ARBORETUM

A beautiful forest setting created by the LSU School of Landscape Architecture

11855 Highland Road, Baton Rouge
225-767-0916 l
su.edu/hilltop/index.php – hilltop@lsu.edu
Open 7 days a week, dawn to dusk

Highland Road is a well-used thoroughfare familiar to millions of LSU fans as the road to Tiger Stadium, home of their beloved Bayou Bengals football team. Yet most attendees are probably not aware that they're passing within yards of a beautiful forest setting created and maintained by LSU's Robert Reich School of Landscape Architecture.

After you turn off Highland Road, about 300 feet along, there's a large gravel parking lot and the first thing you'll see on your left are plants for sale. This tradition was started by the Smith family, the creators of this bucolic setting – they used to bring the plants they had gathered from around the state and leave them for people to take for free. Nowadays the plants are for sale, with the proceeds going toward the upkeep of the arboretum. They are available on the honor system, a personal touch that permeates the grounds.

As you drive a little further into the parking area, you'll be struck by a modern structure (a multi-use administration and education facility) that dominates the entrance to the arboretum. Although nature is the draw, the hand of people is evident, not only in the dramatic buildings

used as classrooms and meeting spaces, but in the well-maintained trails and clearly marked trees and plants. The arboretum has a welcoming atmosphere in which visitors can amble at their own pace and enjoy nature.

The complex includes an open-air pavilion whose design is reminiscent of a Louisiana fishing camp. The Imogene Newsom Brown Educational Facility will be the first LSU building to be registered with the U.S. Green Building Council for possible Leadership in Energy and Environmental Design (LEED). The new buildings will be used by the LSU College of Art and Design to teach green building principles.

The arboretum, dubbed "the cathedral" because of its forest canopy, has many charms. Fallen trees are used as benches for children not only to sit on but to walk across. The ravines, lawns, well-worn artisan-style benches and a wide pond that fans out from a large pavilion attached to the buildings all give a manicured touch to the tranquility that allows for a very pleasant walk.

As you explore the trails, you'll come across paths that are well-worn entrances located only feet away from the upscale subdivisions that now pepper Highland Road. Near the back of the property, you'll see another clump of homes – the residents enjoy the special perk of having an almost private park only steps away from their property.

The journey that led to this special place started with Emory and Annette Smith's move from downtown Baton Rouge to find a more peaceful place to live. Emory soon began traveling the state with friends to bring back native Louisiana plants. Children were drawn to the property, and Emory started to label the plants for the children. Today, one of the special features of the arboretum is its clearly marked plants.

34

HEADSTONE OF
MICHAEL B. BROWN

One of the strangest and most mysterious headstone carvings you're ever likely to see

Springfield Cemetery, Springfield
Right off Louisiana Highway 42 (Main Street), not far from junction of Highways 42 and 22
Every day from dawn to dusk

In a small rural cemetery in Springfield sits one of the strangest and most mysterious headstone carvings one is likely to see anywhere. Right off Louisiana Highway 42 is the last resting place of Michael B. Brown, a 15-year-old boy who was the victim of a hit-and-run driver in August of 1983.

The front of the headstone facing away from the roadway is traditional, but on the back is a scene of what appears to be a traffic accident: In a childish stick-figure style, it might seem to describe the incident that led to Michael's death. At first glance, you might mistake it for a marks-a-lot sketch, but on closer examination you'll see that it's carved into the back of the stone. If the sun is shining, you could miss the engraving as the bright sunlight can wash out the image. The artwork is primitive and childlike, and because it gives names and dates and street signs, this leads many to believe that the artist was trying to solve (or

at least give a clue about) the guilty parties. This is where the legend – and the trouble – started. According to the legend, Michael's mother came back to the grave on the day of his funeral and found the unusual engraving on the back of the headstone: It was believed by some to be Michael identifying his alleged assailant from the great beyond.

Although there is a much simpler explanation backed up by the family, and which debunks the supernatural origins of the carving (see below), the legend grew and has become a modern myth. People would come into the cemetery at night and leave copious amounts of trash – candy wrappers, beer cans, chip bags. They would also vandalize the headstone by knocking it over and breaking objects left by Michael's family.

So strong was the legend that, even when his family members were at the grave to set people straight with the true story, they were not believed. Consequently, people keep coming.

The City of Springfield has had to pass an ordinance to close the cemetery from 6pm to 8am, and many summons have been handed out to transgressors.

The true story

The artwork on the back of the headstone is indeed a childhood drawing that Michael made on a plain brown grocery bag when he was younger. His mother asked Louisiana Memorial to etch it into the back of the stone. They initially forgot but later brought the headstone back to their workshops and etched the scene onto the back, and that is how it comes to be there.

HUNGARIAN SETTLEMENT MUSEUM

35

A thriving Hungarian agricultural community revolving around the strawberry

27455 Louisiana Highway 43, Albany
225-294-5732 – hungarianmuseum.com
Tue 10am–4pm, 2nd & 4th Sat 10am–4pm
By appointment for groups and schools
Free but donations welcome

A small white wooden building with distinctive tin-roofed triangular vestibules, which once housed a community school, is now the home of the Hungarian Settlement Museum. The place is dedicated to a robust Hungarian presence in rural southeastern Louisiana, a fact that flies under most people's radar.

This small yet meticulously and lovingly kept museum is dedicated to preserving the history of Hungarian immigrants – a movement that started with three men in search of a better life for their families, hoping to escape the brutal conditions in the mines and factories of the U.S. North. Their move wound up with hundreds of Hungarian families and thousands of descendants, and the founding of a place dubbed Arpadahon, named for a Hungarian hero circa 896 CE who united the Magyars in what became Hungary. At some point, "Arpadahon" became simply the "Hungarian Settlement," the name by which it is known today.

The agrarian area of southeastern Louisiana offered a chance to live life

as the settlers had known it in Hungary. And there was also the promise of cheap land via the Breckenridge Lumber Company, which clear-cut the area with no intention of reforesting. The company put ads in Hungarian-language newspapers in the northern U.S. and Canada, offering affordable 20-acre parcels. That lured Hungarians to southeastern Louisiana. Hungarian Settlement today is the largest rural Hungarian community in the United States.

The many people who answered this call ended up as an integral part of what became a thriving agricultural community revolving around the strawberry. The product of their labors is celebrated with the annual Strawberry Festival in Ponchatoula, which even in festival-crazy Louisiana is a standout. The museum has exhibits describing the whys and wherefores of strawberry farming and the Hungarian contribution to its success.

Today the Hungarian Settlement Museum is lovingly maintained by docents who are descendants of the first settlers. Most of the objects have been donated through the Hungarian roots of the community. You'll find maps of Hungary, along with traditional Hungarian costumes, wedding dresses, porcelain, musical instruments such as the cimbalom and zither, tributes to the 1956 Hungarian uprising against Soviet rule, and even a Rubik's Cube, the brainchild of a Hungarian and an example of the proud connection that descendants of the first Hungarians in southern Louisiana still have with their ancestry and homeland.

There is also a small but rich archive of personal histories and research documents tucked into a corner library space. It covers a wide range of topics, including the essential role played by the two church communities – one Catholic, the other Presbyterian – in keeping the settlement united and prosperous.

INDEPENDENCE ITALIAN CULTURAL MUSEUM

Memories of Sicilian immigrants

524 Pine Street, Independence
985 878 3773
indymuseum.org
Sat 10:30am–2:30pm, weekdays by appointment

Housed in the former Mater Dolorosa Catholic Church, the Independence Italian Cultural Museum is a visually busy space that appears to be in a constant state of evolution – it is dedicated to the tight-knit family traditions of Italy.

The overwhelming majority of Italian immigrants to southern Louisiana came from Sicily and the museum serves to illustrate the strong links that these settlers still maintain with their beloved homeland.

Independence was a popular destination for Sicilian immigrants coming to America in search of an agricultural setting and a chance at the American dream.

Today, Italians are one of the most prevalent European ancestries in southern Louisiana. New Orleans, only 75 miles from Independence, has a large population of people of Italian descent with an overwhelmingly Sicilian ancestry. An old New Orleans phone book would reveal surnames that correspond to almost every city and town in Sicily.

The museum has a copy of the Our Father written in Sicilian and displayed along with other eye-catching exhibits such as a colorful, authentic Sicilian cart, or *carretto*, built by a local craftsman with local references painted on the sides, as is the custom in the old country.

One of the newer contributions to the museum is a *friscalettu*, a Sicilian reed flute that was carved by the same artisan as the *carretto*. The wood imported from Sicily from which the flute was carved not only gives an authentic sound but is a testament to the care taken by such ethnic museums to respect family ties and the importance of belonging to a historical thread.

To this end, the interior of the museum is dominated by photographs of the local Italian community, often accompanied by family histories.

The museum holds many festivals throughout the year, including "Cucuzza Day," which celebrates the Italian zucchini-like squash of that name – an instantly recognizable agricultural talisman for those of Sicilian heritage in southern Louisiana.

Sicilian is the oldest Romance language to be spun off from Latin. Linguists consider it not as an Italian dialect but as its own separate language as it predates all other Romance languages by hundreds of years.

The Independence Italian Cultural Museum is one of only two museums that is actively attempting to preserve the Sicilian language in America, the other being in New York City.

CAMP MOORE MUSEUM AND CEMETERY

Most of the soldiers here died of disease

706040 Camp Moore Road, Tangipahoa
985-229-2438
campmoorela.com
Wed–Sat 10am–3pm

Reminding us of Camp Moore – the largest training grounds for Confederate troops in Louisiana during the Civil War – the Camp Moore Museum and Cemetery is a historical gem.

It has a collection of artifacts about the Confederacy, including many rare items such as coinage models, medals, ephemera such as posters, flyers and charts that chronicle the death counts of the soldiers who trained here.

The museum also has many items that were used on a day-to-day basis on the front lines: clothing, games, musical instruments, writing implements, letters, eating utensils, knapsacks, uniforms and, of course, weapons.

One of the more poignant and relevant displays, because so many trained at Camp Moore with the enthusiasm of the young going off to

war, is the primitive nature of the medicines and medical instruments available to fight the diseases that felled so many of those buried here.

Behind the large building housing the museum is a tranquil and dignified 2-acre cemetery that memorializes the men who died here, complete with wooden bridges that cross a small creek bed. At least 800 soldiers perished here, mostly of diseases such as measles, diarrhea and pneumonia. There were two measles outbreaks at Camp Moore.

By the turn of the 20th century, the camp and the cemetery were in disrepair and overgrown: The United Daughters of the Confederacy stepped in and replaced the rotten wooden headstones with the marble ones that sit here today. The refurbished camp was dedicated in 1905.

The train tracks you cross as you drive onto the grounds from Louisiana Highway 51 are the tracks that were here in 1861, bringing recruits for the fight ahead. But they also brought visitors: Friends and family members traveled four hours by train from New Orleans to watch their loved ones' training and bid them farewell before they went off to war.

BRITNEY SPEARS MUSEUM

Britney Spears grew up in Kentwood

204 Avenue East, Kentwood
985-229-4656
explorelouisiana.com/music/britney-spears-museum
museumKW@i-55.com
Tue–Sat 9:30am–3:30pm

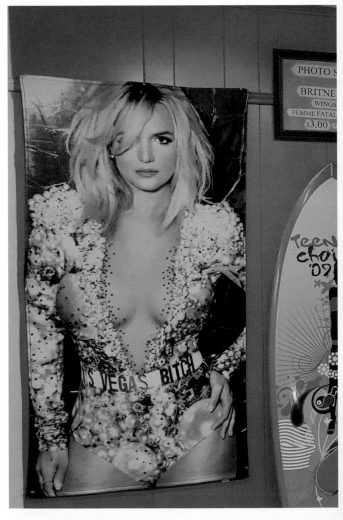

In a former funeral home near the middle of Kentwood, a weary-looking small southern town, the Kentwood Historical & Cultural Museum (better known these days as the Britney Spears Museum) is a repository of small-town America.

Britney Spears, the Princess of Pop, who is given credit for reviving the teen pop genre with her hit albums *Baby One More Time*, and *Oops! ... I Did It Again*, grew up in Kentwood.

Britney took singing and dancing lessons at age 3, performed in local and regional talent shows and was soon on a path to worldwide stardom. She has sold over 100 million albums, six of which were Number 1 sellers. She got her big break after being cast in *The Mickey Mouse Club*, along with other future stars Justin Timberlake and Christina Aguilera, and the rest, as they say, is pop history.

The museum opened in 1995 to honor the men and women of Kentwood who served their country in the armed services and to give an overview of the history of the town – including exhibits on Amos Kent, a lumber baron and the founder of Kentwood. It was later expanded to honor Kentwood's most famous daughter.

The rooms dedicated to Britney are peppered with lots of bright colors, notably pink, and an array of posters, magazines, dolls, and artifacts from her career. The most dramatic item is a pair of wings from her "Femme Fatale" tour – this provides the best photo op for her fans who come and visit. There is also a beautifully done scale model of the set of one of her tours that was made by a fan.

Also of note is a display behind a glass wall of Britney's childhood bedroom, full of all the things a teenage girl might have in her room, including stuffed animals and frilly bed linens.

The tour guide, an accommodating local lady, vouches for the fact that the bedroom features the actual furniture and accouterments of Britney's room when she was growing up in Kentwood. It was donated to the museum by her parents.

Britney is said to have been surprised that someone would want to dedicate a museum to her in her hometown, but she was, indeed, flattered.

Admission is free, donations are accepted, and visitors receive a gift, like a ballpoint pen, to prove they were there. The museum welcomes contributions of memorabilia from fans.

STATUES OF THE APOSTLES

A truly out-of-the-way, under-the-radar attraction

St. Helena Church
122 South 1st Street, Amite
985-748-9057
sthelenachurch.net

Truly out of the way, and very seldom visited, a series of three court-yards at St. Helena Catholic Church in the heart of Amite offers a stunning display of beautiful white resin life-size statues of all 12 of Jesus' apostles. In this small rural town on the north shore of Lake Pontchartrain, this under-the-radar attraction can take your breath away.

Father Mark Beard and the parishioners of St. Helena took eight years to develop this very special place. Smaller replicas of statues found at the Vatican, each statue of the apostles of Christ is depicted with a symbol of how they died or were martyred and stands 6 ft. tall (save St. Peter, who is at the center of the courtyard and is 7 ft. tall).

The location of the statues in Amite was facilitated by, among others, the TV personality Mother Angelica.

Another courtyard is a representation of the Garden of Gethsemane and has a beautiful life-sized statue of Jesus with his hand raised in prayer as well as three other renditions of apostles: These statues were created by the Amite resident Ned Dameron, who also illustrated the covers of the *Dark Tower* series written by Stephen King. They are just as stunning as the apostles in the St. Peter courtyard.

In still another courtyard, the Eucharistic Garden has a large statue of the apostle Paul as a centerpiece with a text providing a perspective of the holy scriptures' Jewish origins.

The courtyards are lit at night and, even though the church and gardens close at the end of the work day, every parishioner has a swipe card that allows access to the grounds 24/7. As Father Beard reminded us, our spiritual needs do not always keep bankers' hours.

Tragically, the driving force behind this special tribute to faith, Father Mark Beard, died in a traffic accident on August 2, 2023. His work and the special displays are lovingly cared for and carried on by members of the congregation.

RELIQUARY
IN ST. HELENA CHURCH

Ten relics from Jesus' crucifixion?

St. Helena Church, Amite – 122 1st Street
985-748-9057 – sthelenachurch.net
Mon–Sat 9am–1pm

At the back of St. Helena Catholic Church in Amite, a very unexpected reliquary (a depository of religious relics in the Catholic Church) officially boasts 151 holy relics, displayed by category and numbered for easy reference. There is an explanatory leaflet on the wall. Each relic is displayed on a circular glass mount.

Supposedly, some of the relics here are from the tomb of Lazarus (resurrected by Jesus), the Cenacle (the room where the Last Supper was held), St. Francis of Assisi and scores of other saints. But most important, ten supposed relics of the crucifixion of Jesus are on display, including some from the crown of thorns and from the wood of the cross.

The relics were obtained from a decommissioned convent in Belgium and were all verified and officially sealed by the Catholic Church in around 2015.

ABITA SPRINGS WATER

Water renowned for its healing powers

22096 Louisiana Highway 36, Abita Springs
Near the roundabout

In the heart of Abita Springs, you'll see a gray concrete cube with four spigots sticking out. Here you can do something that your grandparents probably did: get free spring water renowned for its healing powers.

The ancient raison d'être for the town is the artesian springs that lie below the surface, and if you're in the know, you can still sidle up to the cube and access the water for free. Just walk up to the gray-colored cube and push what appears to be a black plastic button, and the water comes flowing freely and at no charge.

The medicinal quality of the water grew after a story – perhaps apocryphal, perhaps not – of a man of Spanish descent from New Orleans who traveled to the area and met and married a beautiful Choctaw princess. Soon the couple moved back to New Orleans, where the bride fell ill. Her husband sent her back to Abita Springs to take the supposedly available cure from the artesian water that flowed freely in her former home. She was told to drink the water and also to bathe in it – in a month, she was cured! This tale led to the area becoming renowned for its healing water.

> The Choctaw were the first to settle here, and they called the spring *ibetap*, meaning fountain.

ABITA CREEK FLATWOODS PRESERVE

Carnivorous plants that dominate the area

Louisiana Highway 433
225-338-1040
alltrails.com/trail/us/louisiana/abita-creek-flatwoods
Open 7 days a week, dawn to dusk
Approx. 5 miles from Abita Springs

On a quiet country road amidst the pines, only minutes from the traffic roundabout (one of the few in Louisiana), in the heart of Abita Springs, you'll come across a white sign just off Louisiana High-

way 433 that reads "Abita Creek Flatwoods Preserve." A small driveway entrance is blocked by a gate, with room for a half-dozen cars at most.

As you go in through the gate, you'll find a sturdy yet weathered 1,200-ft.-long wooden boardwalk that winds its way through a former Louisiana pine forest. At certain times of the year, notably when spring is in full bloom, you'll be struck by the unusual plants found here. Ten educational signs along the way explain the terrain, the flora and fauna, and the importance of this disappearing habitat.

The flatwood wetlands are part of a major project by the Nature Conservancy to save this type of habitat because only 1% to 5% of the original flora and fauna remains. Volunteers, notably a group dubbed "The Chainsaw Gang," have constructed the boardwalk and the property in conjunction with the Nature Conservancy. This preserve is part of a larger area of sporadic wooded areas that are also part of the privately owned land surrounding the preserve.

Abita Creek Flatwoods Preserve is home to many rare plant species, including Spring Hill flax and little leaf milkroot, only found here in Louisiana. Among the rare fauna found on this 7-mile trail are the endangered gopher tortoise, flower beetle and Flatwoods Digger crawfish, whose distinctive mounds are visible from the walkway. The rare Bach's sparrow and Henslow's sparrow also live in this unique habitat.

However, the preserve's greatest claim to fame, and its most unusual inhabitants, are the various carnivorous plants, a showcase of the wonders of evolution in this area. The most visible is the yellow pitcherplant with its cone-shaped body and a flap at the top to help trap the unsuspecting insects that enter but cannot escape. Other carnivorous plants found here are parrot pitchers and sundews.

One of the instructional graphics near the end of the wooden walkway (which allows visitors to traverse the habitat without getting their feet wet) explains the use of the wood and other resources that led to the area becoming a prime lumber enterprise. Every two or three years there are controlled fires to clear the underbrush, allowing the rare plants to thrive.

ST. JOSEPH'S ABBEY

Founded to educate native-born priests

75376 River Road, St. Benedict
985-892-1800
saintjosephabbey.com
Mon–Sat 9am–11am and noon–4pm, Sun noon–2pm

Deep in the pine woods north of Covington, hidden in plain sight, you'll find a peaceful, contemplative campus dedicated to a religious vocation. Turn off of River Road, then drive across the Bogue Falaya over a one-lane bridge and you'll reach St. Joseph's Abbey, a seminary founded in 1889 that has much to offer to visitors who stumble across it. The

public are welcome to join the monks for mass and morning prayers, and also for vespers.

The campus is dominated by the beautiful Romanesque-style church, built in 1929. Inside the church, you'll find the luxuriously rich murals commissioned by the abbot in 1946 and painted by a Dutch monk, Dom Gregory de Wit, whose works adorn religious buildings in Europe and other places in the United States. Dom Gregory had to find a paint that would withstand the humid atmospheric conditions of southern Louisiana. His stunning works speak to his success in that endeavor.

From the beginning, St. Joseph's has been a place to train and form men for the priesthood. In 1889, when it was founded, the diocese of New Orleans supplied the priests. At that time, most if not all of them were foreign-born. St. Joseph's was founded to educate native-born priests.

The seminary historically consisted of a four-year high school followed by two years of college, and then the students would move on to a major seminary. Today there is an undergraduate college offering a bachelor's degree in Liberal Arts.

St. Joseph's also runs a thriving retreat for individuals and couples, art classes, and a cemetery with plots available to the public.

In the early 21st century, the abbey obtained a Dobson Pipe Organ Opus 2000: Musicians came from all over to play the instrument and make recordings.

Casket business

After Hurricane Katrina in 2005, when thousands of trees were blown down in the area, the abbey started to repurpose the wood by building caskets to raise money to cover the cost of education and health care services for the monks. St. Joseph's became known for its simple mahogany and cypress caskets, and individuals were allowed to order them. However, just as the enterprise was poised to prosper, the Louisiana Board of Funeral Directors tried to quash it – apparently, it was against the law for anyone but a licensed funeral director to sell a burial casket in Louisiana. This led to a court case: St. Joseph's Abbey vs Castile. The 5th Circuit Court of Appeals ruled in favor of the monks, and the casket business continues today.

H.J. SMITH & SONS GENERAL STORE AND MUSEUM

A time capsule

308 North Columbia Street, Covington
985-892-0460
visitthenorthshore.com/listing/h-j-smith-%26-sons-general-store-and-museum/356
Mon, Tue, Thurs & Fri 8:30am–5pm, Wed 8:30–noon, Sat 8:30am–1pm (closed Sun)

Family-owned and -operated since 1876, the H.J. Smith & Sons General Store is a delightful capsule of the past expressed through hardware. The old wooden wagon outside the store is a clue to the small museum-like space that sits to the right of the entrance. At first you may not see the museum for all the clutter of the working hardware store, but if you look down at the wooden floor you'll see a trail of imprinted white cougar prints leading to the hidden repository of the past. The creaky floorboards add an extra audio element to the experience. Once inside, you'll feel as if you're in an attic or a time capsule. There are hundred-year-old products, bottles, and various other odds and ends: a large 20-ft. cypress dugout canoe, a hand-operated washing machine, a wooden boat in the center, old bicycles hanging from the ceiling, a cast iron funeral

casket with a window for the face used during the Yellow Fever epidemics that raged from the late 19th century to 1905, a vintage iron water heater from over a century ago, a 1920s gas pump, and an uncountable array of old stuff, including a petrified rat on your left as you walk in. H.J. Smith's opened in 1876 and has seen seven generations of the same family, who still run the hardware store, which is chock-full of items both familiar and curious. The present owner said in a TV interview that his grandfathers never threw anything away, and it seems that must be true when you see all the things stuffed into the space. There is even a human skeleton that has its own back story. In the same TV interview, Mr. Smith, the present proprietor, explained that although the skeleton used to be kept in the back of the premises, children were fascinated by it: Over the years, the owners decided to put it in a more prominent space to satisfy popular demand. In the 19th century, the skeleton was used by a local Knights of Pythias chapter in initiation ceremonies: It is believed that a local sheriff provided the skeleton.

"If we don't have it, you don't need it"

One of Mr. Smith's grandfathers had a saying that he applied to the contents of his hardware business: "If we don't have it, you don't need it."

Greater New Orleans

ARTHUR CHEVROLET GRACE MEMORIAL

The gravesite of a man who lent his surname to a famous brand

Our Lady of Lourdes Cemetery
100 Canulette Road, Slidell
30 miles from New Orleans

In a somewhat inconspicuous spot, the simple headstone in front of a tree at Our Lady of Lourdes Cemetery in Slidell is a forgotten memorial to a pioneer of automotive racing and design who lent his surname to one of America's foremost and most iconic brands.

The body of Arthur Chevrolet, one of the three brothers who started the Chevrolet Motor Company in 1911, per his wishes, rests in an unmarked grave in Our Lady of Lourdes Cemetery.

The headstone, which for years mistakenly sat in an Indiana cemetery honoring notable contributors to the Indianapolis Speedway, was moved to Slidell in 2017 after a scholar discovered in 2011 that Chevrolet was buried here in Slidell. The graves of the other Chevrolet brothers sit rather inconspicuously in Holy Cross Cemetery in Indianapolis. The Arthur Chevrolet buried in Indianapolis is Arthur Jr.

The elder Arthur Chevrolet moved to the United States from his native Switzerland to join his two brothers, also pioneering race car drivers. He took part in the first Indianapolis 500. His brother Gaston won the Indianapolis 500 in 1916, only to perish in another race that same year.

Arthur Chevrolet had a falling-out with his brother Louis and moved to New Orleans to design and build airplane engines for Andrew Higgins, inventor of the Higgins Boat of World War II fame. Arthur stayed in the New Orleans area to work on other Higgins endeavors. Among his duties, he evaluated PT boats in Lake Pontchartrain for Higgins.

Arthur's life took a couple of unfortunate turns as he entered his sixties: his grandson drowned and his wife was battling dementia. At some point, he slipped into a deep depression and, before his family could intervene, he took his life at the age of 62.

JAYNE MANSFIELD'S DEATH SITE

A full-fledged American sex symbol

Westbound lane near Marina about a mile from Fort Pike on Louisiana Highway 90, Slidell

Hidden from casual view as you drive down Louisiana Highway 90 (even if you seek it out, it's hard to locate without precise directions) is a memorial to one of the most gruesome celebrity deaths of the 20th century. On the side of the highway, about a mile inside Orleans Parish near Slidell, three white wooden crosses mark the spot where the actress Jayne Mansfield and two passengers in her Buick died on June 29, 1967.

The memorial – not unlike any number of do-it-yourself white cross remembrances that grace the sides of American highways – remembers Jayne Mansfield, her driver Ronald B. Harrison, and her boyfriend at the time, Samuel S. Brody, with large lettering.

Three of Mansfield's children, including Mariska Hargitay (who went on to become a star on the TV series Law & Order), were asleep in the backseat – they all survived the crash.

Mansfield and her party were driving from Biloxi, where she had just made a personal appearance at a nightclub, and were on their way to New Orleans for a TV interview when they slammed into the back of a large semi-truck. The collision sheared off the top of the 1966 Buick Electra. Harrison was driving; all three adults in the Buick died almost instantaneously.

The accident was front-page news across the United States. Mansfield was a full-fledged American sex symbol who had had a well-known rivalry with the reigning Hollywood sex symbol, Marilyn Monroe, who tragically died five years before Mansfield.

Mansfield bars

The accident had far-reaching ramifications as the National Highway Traffic Safety Administration, finding that the accident need not have been fatal, ordered all semi-trailer trucks to install a steel bar at the rear to prevent such accidents in the future. These bars hang from the back end of all semi-trucks today. The official name of the bars is Rear Underrun Protection System, but they are also known as Mansfield bars.

Although there were rumors that Mansfield had been decapitated, the coroner is on record as saying that this is untrue.

NORTHLAKE NATURE CENTER

The original habitat of the parish

23135 US-190 Mandeville
985-626-1238
northlakenature.org
Dawn to dusk 7 days a week
Free entry

St. Tammany Parish, just 45 minutes north of New Orleans, is one of the fastest growing suburbs in the United States. It has seen explosive suburban growth in the past 40 years, yet the Northlake Nature Center, located just east of the city of Mandeville, sits veiled from view, preserving the natural feel of the area and transporting the visitor back into the original habitat of the parish.

After parking your car in the small parking lot and walking a few feet into the trees, you experience three different eco-systems: hardwood forests, pine-hardwood forests and pond swamp. These are all accessible by modern boardwalks, with overlooks and interpretive signs along trails.

A new pavilion finished in 1998 gives entrée into this primitive world and facilitates educational activities.

Trails cover nearly seven miles of the 400-acre preserve, bringing you into the heart of a Louisiana wetland. There is a grove of southern magnolias, a cypress/gum swamp and a pond created by beavers, including a lodge visible from a scenic overlook. The spot teems with natural life: indigenous plants, animals and numerous bird species ranging from ducks to songbirds and even a resident flock of wild turkeys. Bayou Castine bounds the nature preserve on the west.

One of the most notable activities at the center each year is BirdFest. This happens in spring, when Louisiana's geographic location on the migration paths for birds returning to North America from wintering in Mexico and South America lends itself to some of the finer birding in the country.

There is also a human element present here. Archaeologists have found remnants of a 700-year-old Acolipissa Native American population that called this site home. Ruins of a more recent vintage can be seen in the guise of a golf course abandoned in the 1930s when its benefactor at the time, Governor Leche, was convicted and sent to prison.

The Northlake Nature Center was established in 1982 by a nonprofit organization to preserve, study and exhibit the natural and cultural resources of Southeast Louisiana and the Florida Parishes (parishes just north of New Orleans so named because they once belonged to the Republic of West Floridan, a short-lived sovereign state, see p. 202).

DEW DROP SOCIAL
& BENEVOLENT JAZZ HALL

The oldest intact jazz hall in the world

438 Lamarque Street
Mandeville
dewdropjazzhall@hotmail.com
dewdropjazzhall.com

The Dew Drop Social & Benevolent Jazz Hall is an old, weathered, unpainted wooden building surrounded by moss-covered oaks on Lamarque Street in the old part of Mandeville. It looks every bit the abandoned rural southern church, but it is arguably one of the most historically significant music venues in America.

Most of the year it is locked down. Sitting idle, it appears like a southern gothic canvas out of central casting. But for a dozen or so times a year, it comes alive to fulfill its original purpose as a place to perform concerts and listen to the joyful noise of jazz.

The Dew Drop Benevolent Society was created in 1885 by civic-minded African Americans to fill a need in the their community for services not available through insurance. The society's goals were to care for the sick, to provide food and housing and to offer financial assistance for members in need.

In 1895, a cornerstone was laid. The present day building opened the same year, making the Dew Drop Social and Benevolent Jazz Hall the oldest intact jazz hall in the world.

Almost immediately after its opening, jazz musicians from New Orleans started to sail across Lake Pontchartrain from the resorts on the south shore, where jazz was flourishing and evolving.

Virtually every jazz great of that time is purported to have traveled to Mandeville, then a thriving resort, to play the music that would soon take the world by storm. The likes of Kid Ory, Buck Johnson, Papa Celestin, George Lewis, Buddy Pettit and Louis Armstrong came here to play. They played not only for the crowds, but also for themselves, in an environment where they could experiment and let loose, refining their sound for the outside world.

Dew Drop lore claims that Armstrong would slip back into Mandeville during the 30s and 40s to escape the pressure of his growing global celebrity, to recharge his energy and to stay connected to his musical roots.

In the 1940s, African American business began to succeed and the need for benvolent societies began to wane. The original community leaders who started the Dew Drop passed on and the building became almost abandoned, sitting unused for nearly 60 years.

In 2007, with impetus from the National Park Service, New Orleans Jazz Commission, the George Buck Foundation, and the City Of Mandeville, the venue was brought back into use and the sounds of traditional jazz were once again heard in the small music hall.

Today, proceeds from all events go to preserve and restore the hall and to support music education.

SEVEN SISTERS OAK

*Limbs twisting high and wide in a pose akin
to interpretive dance*

200 Fountain Street, Lewisburg
lgcfinc.org/live-oak-society.html

I n Lewisburg, a suburb of Mandeville near the shore of Lake Pontchartrain, the limbs of a magnificent live oak tree reach upward and outward, twisting high and wide, as if seeking something. In a pose akin to interpretive dance, it stands in the place it has occupied for perhaps a thousand years or more.

At 67 feet high and 130 feet in diameter, with a girth last measured at nearly 40 feet, the Seven Sisters Oak is the largest live oak in the south. Estimated to be between 500 and 1500 years old, it holds the title of National Champion Live Oak and has been designated the President of the Live Oak Society (whose members are all trees), an honor it has held since 1968.

Located on private property, the oak was a matter of disputed authenticity for a time as many claimed it was actually not one but perhaps several oaks that had grown together over the years to appear as one tree.

However, in 1976 all doubt was dispelled when a team of federal foresters inspected the tree and found a single root system.

The name Seven Sisters has several origin stories. One says the tree is named for its seven limbs, although there are actually more than seven branches extending out and up. Another claims that the owners of the property on which the oak stands had seven daughters, hence the Seven Sisters appellation. Yet another claims it is derived from a Choctaw name lost to history.

Lewisburg sits on the banks of Lake Pontchartrain, to the left after you cross the Causeway from New Orleans. It is a tiny, lesser-known and lesser-traveled part of Mandeville. Although it has been there for many years, it remains something of a secret, as even many Orleanians who are asked to locate it are at a loss. This also adds to the relative obscurity of this huge and important tree.

Originally Choctaw land, Lewisburg is an historic property. Catholic Father Adrien-Emmanuel Rouquette, the first native of Louisiana to be ordained a priest, sermonized and converted many of the Native Americans with whom he had enjoyed a close relationship since his childhood. He was known to have attempted to translate the Bible into Choctaw and indeed was bestowed the Choctaw name *Chata-Ima* (Choctaw-like). In this area, perhaps under the canopy of this very tree, he is believed to have ministered to his newly converted flock.

MAHALIA JACKSON'S GRAVESITE ⑥

The overlooked tomb of one of the giants of American music

Providence Memorial Park & Mausoleum, Metairie
8200 Airline Drive
504-464-0541
providenceparknola.com
Office hours: Tues–Fri 9am–2pm (by appointment only)
12 miles from New Orleans

In a corner of the Providence Memorial Park & Mausoleum, standing alone, is a simple yet elegant tomb that can easily be seen from Airline Drive. Thousands drive by every day, but the grave is almost anonymous. This is the final resting place of one of the giants of American music, Mahalia Jackson. The grave is right next to the mausoleum but is in its own separate space, which means that admirers can easily walk up to pay their respects.

Born in New Orleans, Mahalia Jackson found her final resting place in the suburbs in a neighborhood called Bunche Village, named after Ralph Bunche, the first person of African descent to win the Nobel Peace Prize (1950).

The granddaughter of enslaved people and raised in poverty in New Orleans, Jackson was drawn to singing in her church and was influenced

by other New Orleans spiritual music. At the age of 16, she moved north to Chicago, where her incredible voice and presence brought her international fame. And in turn, she influenced many others with her talent and success. She was widely recognized as one of the most influential vocalists of the 20th century and is considered one of if not the greatest gospel singers of all time.

She was such a successful recording artist that she was asked repeatedly to record other genres, but she steadfastly refused (she even turned down a request from Louis Armstrong). In line with a commitment to her faith and a promise she made to God, she only ever recorded gospel music.

Appearing at sold-out concerts all over Europe, Jackson was the first American artist to give a private performance for the Japanese royal family since World War II. She scaled many barriers faced by African American artists in mid-20th-century America – among many "firsts", she was the first gospel singer to appear at Carnegie Hall and the first to give a gospel performance at the Newport Jazz Fest.

Her style has been described as passionate, emotional, improvisational, singular and sometimes frenetic.

She sang at John F. Kennedy's inaugural ball in 1961 and was involved in the civil rights movement as well as being a tireless supporter of the Black community at grassroots level. Although she was active in political and social movements following the assassination of Martin Luther King Jr. (a personal friend and supporter), she subsequently stepped back from giving political or personal endorsements.

GROUCHO'S BERET

An ad hoc museum

Antoine's restaurant
713 St. Louis
504-581-4422
antoines.com
Daily 11:30am–2pm and 5:30pm–9pm
Riverfront streetcar or #5 Marigny-Bywater bus

Antoine's, the oldest restaurant in the United States still under the control of the family that founded it, is truly a museum unto itself. Among the many artifacts, Groucho Marx's beret (the one he wore on his first European tour) is displayed in a glass case surrounded by ashtrays, dinnerware, glasses, bottles and other bric-à-brac. The simple hat, worn by one of the most iconic figures of world cinema and an important figure in American cultural life, may be one of the best-kept secrets in the city. A gift to Antoine's proprietor Roy Alciatore, the dark blue beret is accompanied by a letter from Groucho himself.

Once you get past the traditional main dining room and its old world charm, numerous other dining rooms teem with memorabilia and history. Photos of the famous who have dined there are framed on the walls: Jean Harlow, J. Edgar Hoover and George Patton in one seven-foot square section of wall alone. There are many others throughout the restaurant, including a signed photo of the three Marx Brothers.

The "collection' is a grab bag of cool: glassware from the House of Napoleon, glassware and dinnerware from potentates around the world, an original Edison light bulb, a rare silver duck press (you may bring your own duck), and countless other items can be found here.

Each dining room has its own personality. The Rex Room, for example, is the King of Carnival and his party have a pre-parade meal surrounded by Mardi Gras memorabilia such as costumes, jewelry and ball favors.

Then there is the Proteus Room, the Snail Room, the Japanese Room (closed after Pearl Harbor and not reopened until 1999) and, of course, the Mystery Room. Next to the main dining room, the Mystery Room came by its name during Prohibition. The story goes that during that time, ladies would excuse themselves, enter the adjacent room through the rest room and return with coffee cups filled with liquor. When asked, "Where did you get the beverage?" the ladies would answer simply, "It's a mystery."

The origin of the word "appetizer"

In a large frame in the second dining room, hanging beside photos of celebrities, is the story of how the word "appetizer' was coined. In the early 1950s, the United States Restaurant Association wanted to replace the word hors d'oeuvre, which it considered too European, with a more American appellation. Roy Alciatore, the proprietor of Antoine's at the time, submitted the winning entry, "Appetite Teaser", which became the word "appetizer' we use today.

CAMP PARAPET

The only site left over from the Civil War

Half a block east of the intersection of Causeway Blvd. and Arlington Street
jeffersonhistoricalsociety.com
Open: one Saturday a year in the fall – on Camp Parapet Day
E-5 Causeway bus or E-3 Kenner Local bus

S wallowed up by an aging suburbia just about two football fields away as the crow flies from the Mississippi River in Jefferson Parish (near American Legion Hall 267), Camp Parapet is the only site in the greater New Orleans area left over from the Civil War.

Behind padlocked gates and a chain link fence, the powder magazine the single remaining building of the once extensive military complex – can easily be seen from the street. In 1984, the powder magazine and the immediate surroundings were restored and now serve as a historical reminder of the war for school children and visitors on tours arranged through the Jefferson Historical Society.

Camp Parapet was designed to protect the city from a Union invasion. The fort was originally named Fort John Hunt Morgan after a Kentucky war hero. The Union invasion, however, came from the south when Admiral David Farragut's fleet took the city and the Confederate forces in a panic tried to sabotage the fort. The fortifications fell into the hands of the Union forces and the site was named Camp Parapet. The Union forces garrisoned Camp Parapet for the rest of the war to fend off a Confederate invasion that never came.

The camp once boasted a hot shot furnace, an observatory, a guard house, officers' quarters and nine heavy artillery guns. Now all that remains is a brick enclosed structure in an earthen mound that served as a powder magazine.

Even though it experienced no fighting during the war, the fort can still claim some important historical significance. After the Union took possession of the fortification, freed slaves flocked to the fort in search of food and shelter often with families in tow. Many who came were given jobs as laborers or assistants and many ended up serving under General John Walcott, a strict abolitionist from Vermont.

The 73rd Regiment United States Colored Troops that served at Camp Parapet during the war were the first African American regiment formed in the Union Army. The 73rd regiment famously fought with valor during the Port Hudson campaign. The African American forces at Port Hudson were also the first African American troops who would serve under African American field leadership. One of those officers, P.B.S. Pinchback, later became the first African American to serve as governor of a U.S. state, an event that wouldn't occur again until 1990.

Due to poor hygienic conditions, deaths were so prevalent at the site that it served as a cemetery for 7,000 soldiers who were later moved to Chalmette National Cemetery. The camp has continued to serve as a cemetery for two area church congregations. The facilities left over from the war also served as the Jefferson Parish lockup until the 1920s.

USS *METAIRIE* STENCIL

A faux submarine

3224 West Napoleon Avenue, Metairie

While driving along West Napoleon Avenue near the Causeway Boulevard intersection close to Interstate 10, exit 228, in the unincorporated suburb of Metairie, you might notice a submarine in a residential area. It sits on landlocked real estate on what most people call a median, but in New Orleans they call a neutral ground, and it's not a submarine.

So what is it? Instead of a real submarine transported from a U.S. naval base, it's a submarine-shaped drain cover painted black with USS *Metairie* stenciled on it by some enterprising prankster. You'll do a double take if you notice it as it does actually look like a submarine.

Metairie has many open drainage canals and lots more that are covered by concrete and grass. Here it seems that the faux submarine is covering up one of those drainage canals, and the pipe coming out of the USS *Metairie* is presumably for venting. Here it could be construed as a periscope.

There's no convenient parking spot to take a photo or investigate further; you must park on a side street. As West Napoleon is a busy thoroughfare, take care when crossing the street if you want to get a closer look.

SINGING OAK

Largest wind chime sculpture in America

*On Big Lake in City Park near the intersection of Lelong Avenue
and Wisner Blvd.*
neworleanscitypark.com
Canal streetcar–City Park/Museum
#91 Jackson/Esplanade bus – #90 Carrolton bus

The Singing Oak consists of seven wind chimes, tuned to play as one, hidden inside a 180-year-old oak tree. The largest chime is 14 feet long and the smallest is 30 inches.

As wind blows through the canopy the chimes catch lake breezes coming down Bayou St. John, which serves as one of the park's boundaries.

The chimes are painted black to blend in with the natural shadow of the oaks and are tuned to the major pentatonic scale, the predominant scale used in West African music. It was this music that inspired spirituals, gospel, jazz, blues and even rock 'n' roll.

The flood caused by the failure of the federally maintained levees during Hurricane Katrina inundated the park, damaging or killing many of the trees. Artist Jim Hart created the chimes and placed them in one of the remaining trees in the John S. McIlhilleny Meadow. The meadow is located near the east end of Big Lake.

The seventh most visited urban park in the United States, City Park inhabits a natural fulcrum of New Orleans historic real estate. It is home to the oldest grove of mature live oaks in the world; some of them are said to be 900 years old. Curiously enough, one of the newest attractions at the park is also located in one of these ancient trees.

Indigenous to the southern United States, the live oak ranges from Virginia to Florida in the east and along the gulf coast to Mexico; it is one of the more striking, accessible and ubiquitous natural wonders of New Orleans. Thanks to the foresight of generations of city planners, the city's boulevards are graced by hundreds of stately examples.

Today, this ancient tree serves as a peaceful melodic respite; a place for people to meet, lunch, visit or just contemplate the day.

WAVE OF THE WORLD FOUNTAIN ⑪

A work of art lost for 30 years finally returns

On Big Lake in City Park near the intersection of LeLong Avenue and Wisner Blvd.
neworleanscitypark.com
Canal streetcar–City Park/Museum
#90 Jackson/Esplanade bus, #91 Carrolton bus

At the bank of Big Lake in City Park surrounded by a small forest of reeds, "The Wave of the World" is a fountain sculpted by internationally known artist Lynda Benglis. The intriguing story of this beautiful work is reminiscent of the satirical novel "A Confederacy of Dunces" by John Kennedy Toole, the celebrated work of fiction set in New Orleans.

The fountain has traveled across the Atlantic and back and was exhibited in front of a casino in Monaco just after the 1984 New Orleans World's Fair . Yet it has spent much of the past several decades languishing.

Winner of a competition to create art for the 1984 New Orleans World's Fair under the theme "Fresh Water as a Source of Life", Ms. Benglis' fountain was purchased by businessman Carl Eberts for $100,000 at the behest of his daughters (with a grant of $15,000 that required it to be displayed to the public). After the first blush of ownership, Mr. Eberts was at a loss as to where to display the piece, so he donated it to the city of Kenner. At that point, it disappeared from the consciousness of the city. It was left in a kind of bureaucratic purgatory and became lost for over thirty years. All the while it stood in plain sight in a yard next to the city's sewage treatment plant.

"Nobody knew what it was," said Mike Quigley, Kenner's Chief Administrative Officer. Which begs the question, "how did it get into the unknowing hands of the City of Kenner?".The answer turned out to be that the former mayor of Kenner and later the Parish President of Jefferson Parish, who later ended up in prison for some kind of malfeasance, happened to be Mr Eberts' brother-in-law and it was he who in a burst of civic-mindedness proposed that it be donated to the city. "We didn't know what it was worth," said Kenner mayor Mike Yenni. About a million dollars as it turns out.

Ms. Benglis had inquired about the whereabouts of a work she held dear to her heart. Finally, thanks to her persistance, diligent attorneys, a local art dealer, and the curator of the New Orleans Museum Of Art, the fountain found its way back into the public's consciousness after a detour via Ms. Benglis' studios to be repaired. Now on loan to the park, with the assistance of the New Orleans-based Helis Foundation, the sculpture is again delighting visitors.

LULING MANSION

The most beautiful house in the South

1436 Leda Court
Private residence not open to the public
#91 Jackson/Esplanade bus or Canal–Museum streetcar

At the end of Esplanade Avenue as you approach City Park traveling from the river, the old boulevard sparkles with beautiful mansions, many over a century old. But the star, and once the finest home in New Orleans, lurks just off the avenue obscured from view, even to those who know it's there.

Now a run-down apartment building, the mansion was designed by James Gallier Jr., one of New Orleans' most esteemed architects, and built in 1865 by cotton merchant Florence Luling, all for the princely sum of $24,000 – the equivalent of at least a few million dollars today.

Although it has obviously seen better days, it still boasts a regal bearing with balconies, galleries, arched windows and a large stairway leading to the front door overlooking a lawn that once fronted on Esplanade Avenue. It still has the power to inspire awe when seen by unsuspecting eyes. Modeled after an Italian Renaissance palace, the property once encompassed 80 acres, which included its own lake. Shortly after moving in, the Lulings were struck with tragedy when their two sons drowned in Bayou St. John only a few blocks away. They left New Orleans never to return and sold the property to the Louisiana Jockey Club, which had just purchased the adjacent Creole Racetrack. The club opened the Fair Grounds Racetrack the next year in 1872.

The Jockey Club became a legendary party destination, with lavish banquets, carnival masquerades and what were described as extravagant cocktail parties. These social affairs were attended by a who's who of New Orleans society as well as important dignitaries visiting the city.

The notables included Ulysses S. Grant, Edgar Degas and Grand Duke Alexis of Russia. The Jockey Club sold the property in 1905, citing the expense of the upkeep. It was converted into eight apartments, some of which are still in use. Today, the old grand dame of a building stands a bit pared back. Some of its outbuildings are gone and much of the luxurious grounds of yesteryear have been sold. The once extensive parcel of land was subdivided into residential lots, some of which now serve to shield its view from the passing traffic.

But the mansion itself remains, in all its crumbling glory, as a proud reminder of a different age.

RESIDENCE ON ESPLANADE AVE., NEW ORLEANS, LA.

POPP'S FOUNTAIN

A spectacular 30-foot spray in the air

12 Magnolia Drive
504-482-4888
neworleanscitypark.com
10am–10pm
#45 Lakeview bus (closest public transit)

At this rarely visited landmark in the less traveled northern side of City Park, the sound of Popp's Fountain's multiple water plumes competes with the constant whirr of automobiles on the busy interstate highway only steps away.

A 60-foot circular fountain built in 1937 by the WPA, Popp's Fountain is surrounded by 26 Corinthian columns connected at the top by a wooden trellis adorned with flowing foliage. It has seen its ups and downs since its inception, but today it has new life: The 12-acre park in which it stands has been fully renovated and landscaped with plants, shrubs and native trees, creating a lush contemplative space. The newly constructed Arbor Room makes it a perfect site for events such as weddings.

Featuring leaping dolphins around a metal lotus centerpiece designed by Enrique Alferez, the Art Deco fountain shoots a spectacular 30-foot spray into the air.

For all its beauty and efforts to refurbish and update it, the spot remains a quiet refuge in the park on most days. Visitors will often find themselves alone, or one of very few, on any given day.

The fountain was first funded by Rebecca Grant Popp and her sister, with a donation of $25,000 in 1929, to honor Mrs. Popp's husband, who died an untimely death. The fountain is named in Mr. Popp's memory. The original plan for the monument was created by the Olmstead Brothers in 1929.

Witchcraft in the fountain

In the 1970s, the fountain was so neglected that it became a spot used by a local witch to hold rituals. Popp's Fountain in those days was derelict, unfenced and open. Local witch Mary Oneida practiced meditation in the area and eventually used the 60-foot circular fountain with its tiered walkways for witchcraft ceremonies. The coven led by Ms. Oneida, The Religious Order of Witchcraft, was the first to be recognized as a 'church' by the state of Louisiana. Ms. Oneida died in 1981, but some say that strange things still occur at the fountain.

MUSIC TREE

A totem to the renewal of New Orleans

On the bank of Bayou St. John near the intersection of Moss Street and Orleans Avenue
Canal streetcar or #91 Jackson/Esplanade bus

At the south end of Bayou St. John, near to its intersection with Orleans Avenue, a dead oak tree has become a work of art. It is the work of master chainsaw artist Marlin Miller, who has created similar works all over the United States. The tree sports a keyboard on its trunk, a fiddle and a guitar on one side, and a pelican on another. Miller chose to preserve the narrow branches at the top of the tree by carving birds in flight.

After the initial shaping of the tree, he burnishes the surface with a torch to add depth and then varnishes it; the varnish seeps into the tree to preserve both the image and the wood itself. Finally, it is treated to protect it from termites.

Miller receives numerous requests to apply his magic to trees, so he must pick and choose his subjects carefully. He has specific criteria that a tree must meet to qualify for his beautiful makeovers: It must be hardwood; it must be on public property; it must be in a highly visible area; and it must have some emotion tied to it. Miller said that the tree at the end of Bayou St. John met all of these requirements "perfectly".

This tree, called the "Music Tree", actually survived the wind and flooding of Katrina only to succumb to a lightning strike during Hurricane Isaac in 2012.

The artful transformation of the tree was at the behest of organizers of the Mid-City Bayou Boogaloo, a free neighborhood music and arts festival, wishing to focus attention on the replanting of trees along the bayou.

Proceeds from the festival have gone toward repopulating the bayou with trees lost to time and hurricanes.

The tree stands as a solitary sentinel all year round, except for one weekend when the shores of the bayou become a fairground for a free music festival.

CELTIC CROSS

A testament to thousands of Irish immigrants

West End Blvd. and Down Street on the neutral ground
24 hours daily
#45 Lakeview bus or Canal–Cemeteries streetcar then transfer to #45 Lakeview bus

From hallowed ground in the middle of the prosperous middle class neighborhood of Lakeview, a lone Kilkenny marble cross looks out into the vast New Orleans neutral ground of West End Boulevard, upon hallowed ground in the middle of the prosperous middle class neighborhood of Lakeview. It stands as, a testament to the thousands of Irish immigrants who built the New Basin Canal at great cost in suffering and lives.

The site of the Celtic cross at the West End has recently been expanded to include a four-acre interpretive park provided by the Ancient Order of the Hibernians to celebrate and commemorate the vast and lasting contributions of the Irish community to the culture and history of New Orleans.

The memorial was dedicated in 1990 by the Irish Cultural Society of New Orleans, and the ceremony was attended by the Irish ambassador to the United States to honor the sacrifice of the men who excavated arguably the greatest public works project of 19th-century New Orleans.

The canal was started in 1832 and it took six years to build the shipping channel route that was meant to compete with the Carondelet Canal, a major portal for trade between Lake Pontchartrain and the Creole section of the city. The New Basin Canal would connect the lake to the Faubourg St. Mary (which now is the Central Business District), and was conceived to take advantage of the booming economy of the American sector, which was emerging as the financial powerhouse of the city. Schooners brought produce, lumber, bricks and commodities of all kinds that tied New Orleans into the economy of the entire region. The canal was in fact a tremendous financial success and contributed to the flourishing growth of the city's economy for almost a hundred years.

The canal was filled in after World War II, and its route was incorporated in the building of the Pontchartrain Expressway in the 1960s, which is now part of the U.S. Interstate Highway System.

Thousands of Irish immigrants dug through an unforgiving cypress swamp to create the canal. Slave labor, readily available at the time, was not utilized because of the dangerous working conditions, for the slaves' lives were deemed more valuable than that the lives of immigrant laborers. Yellow fever, cholera and malaria, along with brutal working conditions, claimed anywhere from 6,000 to 30,000 lives of workers from the Emerald Isle – and all for the wage of one dollar a day.

Such were the conditions that many died where they stood and were buried in the levees of the canal or in the mud and shells of the roadways where they fell. Thousands were given neither last rites nor grave markers.

HIGGINS THERMO-CON HOME

Thermo-Con, touted as a modern wonder material

30 Tern Street
Private residence, not open to the public
#45 Lakeview bus

Literally only a couple of hundred yards from Lake Pontchartrain, a white International Style mansion sitting off the beaten path in an exclusive nook of Lake Vista is one of the few tangible reminders of a failed experiment by one of New Orleans' more storied entrepreneurs.

Built by Andrew Higgins as his personal residence, the house was designed to showcase his invention Thermo-Con, a modern building material he hoped would revolutionize construction post-World War II.

Recent owners of the home have done much upkeep, scrupulously adhering to Higgins' vision.

They have been greatly assisted by the fact that the home came with a complete set of original plans. Original materials have been used whenever possible and finer details, such as the mahogany doors and double helix interior staircase, have been preserved. Also still present is a wet bar that Higgins installed, fashioned out of the stern of an LCVP landing craft that hit the beach at Normandy.

From all accounts by occupants of the home over the years, Thermo-Con has delivered on its promise of strength, durability and insulation.

Thermo-Con, touted as a modern wonder material, was a combination of Portland cement, water, aluminum flakes, caustic soda and bituminous emulsion. The mixture was poured into a mold and would rise in a process similar to baking. This process produced a gas-expanded cellular composition with a very high strength-to-weight ratio. Thermo-Con was fire-resistant, moisture-proof and vermin-proof, with low heat and cold transmission and high heat insulation properties.

Another advantage was that it boasted wood-like characteristics, making it extremely versatile. All these positive selling points enticed the U.S. Army to sign a contract with Higgins' corporation to build prototypes, in order to develop a standard house design to meet the army's housing shortage. But the idea never caught on and very few structures built with Thermo-Con remain. One that has survived is at Fort Belvoir in Virginia: It still houses visiting dignitaries and was designated a historic landmark by the state of Virginia.

Andrew Higgins was also the founder of Higgins Industries, the New Orleans-based manufacturer of the Higgins boat (LCVP) during World War II. General Dwight D. Eisenhower once proclaimed him as the man who won World War II because of the importance of his landing boats, built in New Orleans and delivered to soldiers in battle, including the Normandy landing on D-Day.

LOUP GAROU STATUE

Unapologetic in all regards... honest, coarse, ugly and powerful

2000 Lakeshore Drive
504-280-6000
uno.edu
#52 St. Bernard-Paris bus or #55 Elysian Fields bus

At nearly 104 tons and 33 feet high, a massive concrete sculpture seems unlikely to be considered a secret. Nonetheless, Peter Lundberg's thrice-named work "Loup Garou," standing for all to see on the University of New Orleans (UNO) campus across the street from the Fine Arts Gallery, fits the bill.

UNO is situated on Lake Pontchartrain and is thereby not one of the more visited parts of the city. The placement of the huge work of art finds it in one of the least traversed parts of the campus, on a dead end street to boot, that sees little to no automobile traffic on any given day.

Vermont-based sculptor Lundberg created his piece in New Orleans by digging a hole in the backyard of a former molasses plant in Bywater then filling the void first with rebar, tires, industrial cables and miscellaneous debris before adding lots of concrete. An industrial crane raised the massive result, which was then entitled "Mississippi Gateway."

The sculpture was moved to City Park near the New Orleans Museum of Art, but the soft ground at the park proved an unwelcoming host, not allowing for a stable base. For a time, the work laid on its side until it was moved to another destination on UNO's campus. Again its base seemed unstable and it was eventually moved across Harwood Drive to a new custom-made base, where it stands today.

After its latest move, the cost alone of moving the work was approximately $145,000, almost equal to its estimated worth of $150,000. The work was described by one art professor as "unapologetic in all regards... honest, coarse, ugly and powerful."

Lundberg renamed the piece "Mississippi Passage" some time later. His custom in the past has been to name his work after mythological creatures, so after becoming familiar with the French Louisiana werewolf myth of Loup Garou he settled on the present name.

OUR LADY OF LAVANG MISSION

*A postcard in memory of a miracle in the
Vietnamese jungle*

6054 Vermillion Blvd.
504-283-0559
lavangshrine.net
#55 Elysian Fields bus or #51 St. Bernard-St. Anthony bus

Located at the site of a former Lutheran church in a working class neighborhood that was ravaged by hurricane Katrina, Our Lady of La Vang Mission is a Vietnamese shrine standing several stories tall, topped by a statue of Our Lady of LaVang. A raised altar sits above two circular tiered pools of water and occasionally serves in outdoor services of the church that occupies this space. Every Mother's Day, the grounds are also home to the Festival of Our Lady of LaVang.

The site looks as if it belongs on a Vietnamese postcard. Indeed, with mass schedules and most signage clearly in Vietnamese, this church is among several in New Orleans that serve the large Vietnamese community: After the fall of Vietnam in 1976, many Vietnamese fled the communist regime and settled in the United States. There are now approximately two dozen Catholic churches that bear the name of Our Lady of LaVang in the United States. Due to the similarity of the New Orleans climate to their homeland and the proximity of the fishing industry, many Vietnamese found new homes in New Orleans.

Another key reason for the settlement in New Orleans was New Orleans Archbishop Philip Hannan, the first Catholic archbishop to visit Fort Chafee in Arkansas where the first refugees were sent. Through the work of Catholic charities, Archbishop Hannan resettled over 1,000 families on that first trip. In 1974 there were almost zero Vietnamese in the city. Today there are over 15,000. The New Orleans Vietnamese community has flourished in the city and boasts Joseph Cao, the first United States congressman of Vietnamese heritage, as one of their own.

A Vietnamese tree and the apparition of Virgin Mary

The shrine gets its name from an incident deep in the Vietnamese rainforest at the end of the 18th century. The emperor of Annam had issued an anti-Catholic edict and the faithful fled into the forest and congregated at one particular tree every night to pray the rosary. One night up in a branch of that tree, an apparition of a lady dressed in traditional Vietnamese garb and holding an infant in her arms instructed those assembled to boil the leaves of the tree as a medicine to combat illnesses that had befallen them. As word spread, that place became a holy site for Vietnamese Catholics and a chapel was built here to honor Our Lady. Persecutions continued over the years with an estimated 100,000 Catholics being martyred between 1700 and 1800. In Vietnam, the Basilica of Our Lady of La Vang is situated in what is today Hai Phu commune in Hai Lăng District of Quang Tri Province in Central Vietnam. La means "leaf" and Vang means "grass seed".

LAKEFRONT AIRPORT TERMINAL MURALS

A riot of Art Deco design

6001 Stars and Stripes Blvd.
504-243-4010
lakefrontairport.com
Terminal: daily 7am–4:30pm
Wed–Sun 11am–4pm and by appointment
#60 Hayne bus

The striking pastel yellow bas-relief exterior of the New Orleans Lakefront Airport gives only a hint of the opulent interior that awaits the visitor to this time capsule of a building.

The architectural detail seems endless: a marble staircase, chandeliers out of a Dashiell Hammet novel, the geometric patterned inlaid ceiling, a vintage neon sign pointing toward the dining room and stylized metalwork skirting the balcony. Even the coffee shop stools drip with the crisp lines of the era.

A compass in the center of a terrazzo floor points to every corner of the globe and specifically to the Xavier Gonzalez murals that adorn the walls of the balcony, celebrating the history of human flight.

Of the eight murals that were originally created, only seven survive; the eighth canvas, entitled *Flight over Bali*, has been severely damaged.

The murals, depicting famous flights in aviation history, including Admiral Richard Byrd's flight over the South Pole and Lindbergh's groundbreaking flight to Paris, were restored in 2015-16 by experts brought in from all over the country.

One thing you can safely say about Gov. Huey Long, who ruled Louisiana like an emperor in the 1920s and 30s, is that he never thought small, especially when it came to public works. The Louisiana Capitol building, the massive Art Deco Charity Hospital and the Mississippi River Bridge, now named after him, all attest to that. But his ambitions were never more artistically expressed than in the airport that he commissioned and opened in 1934 as a state-of-the-art airline terminal.

Today, the newly restored building at Lakefront Airport is testament to Long's vision: A riot of artistic design, it is thought to be the first modern Art Deco land and sea airport.

Huey Long and his appointed Levee Board president Abe Shushan built the airport on a sliver of reclaimed land jutting out into Lake Pontchartrain. This made for wide views for pilots. It also conveniently placed the glittering terminal and runways just outside New Orleans' jurisdiction. Having feuded with the city's politicians for years, Long's maneuver gave him and his proxy, Shushan, full control. The airport was originally named after Shushan, who had carte blanche to achieve their vision without interference.

The airport served New Orleans as its primary airport from 1934 to 1946, until city fathers had their revenge by building Moisant Airport, 20 miles away in a neighboring parish. However, Lakefront Airport remains one of the busiest general aviation airports in the United States.

ARLENE MERAUX RIVER OBSERVATION CENTER

Quiet bird's eye vantage point over the Mississippi

5124 East St. Bernard Highway
merauxfoundation.org
5 miles from New Orleans

Driving south from New Orleans on East St. Bernard Highway right before you come to the picturesque Docville Oaks, turn right through the archway labeled Docville Farms and you'll see a new red five-story building: the Arlene Meraux River Observation Center (AMROC), which visually dominates the complex of buildings and facilities dedicated to education and the role of agriculture in our everyday lives.

On the fifth level of AMROC, you'll find a quiet, peaceful observation deck looking out over the Mississippi River. Due to the low-lying topography of southern Louisiana and the once overwhelming presence of working wharfs along the river, there are very few high vantage points for the casual observer, making this a rare view.

One of the beauties of the observation deck is its accessibility: Anyone can drive into the park and just climb the stairs or take the elevators up

without any fanfare. This tranquil spot is usually a private perch from which to watch the massive ships from all over the world that ply the waters on their way to New Orleans.

Docville Farms covers 130 acres of a 646-acre parcel of land stretching from the Mississippi River to Lake Borgne. The complex, which is named after Dr Louis "Doc" Meraux, now has an educational mission and there are many unique and interesting attractions. Among them are the Main House, AMROC, the Dave Thompson Event Barn (a renovated structure moved from New Orleans French Market in the 1940s), working stables with livestock, a greenhouse showcasing native plants and their role in combating coastal erosion, sugar cane and citrus cops, and a crawfish pond.

These agricultural "exhibits" are used to teach 3rd- to 6th-grade kids about the role of agriculture in our daily lives. This culminates in a once-a-year event: Organized by LSU Ag School, 4H and other groups, AgMagic is open to the public.

An augmented-reality sandbox

One of the most unique features at Docville is something dubbed an augmented-reality sandbox. Described as a cutting-edge educational instrument, it's a hands-on sandbox and museum experience that teaches kids about geography, hydrology erosion, topography and other natural sciences. How it works is a combination of modern technology and a concept known to children since the dawn of time: hands on. A computer-generated image is projected onto the sand and you just add the kids, who can then build mountains, valleys and watersheds by rearranging the sand, helped along by the projected images.

NEARBY

A tunnel of live oaks

If you continue south on East St. Bernard Highway, you'll immediately come upon another sight just yards past Docville Farm. Right after the

entrance, you'll see the Docville Oaks: a tunnel of live oaks that create a canopy to drive your car through. An almost irresistible south Louisiana photo op.

AMMO MAGAZINES

Abandoned ammo dumps left over from World War II

Woodlands Nature Conservancy
440 F. Edward Hebert Boulevard, Belle Chasse
504-433-4000
info@woodlandsconservancy.org
Dawn to dusk 7 days a week
Bottomlands Trail: a 5.5-mile round trip
10 miles from New Orleans

At the end of a well-maintained nature trail on New Orleans' West Bank, inside the Woodlands Nature Conservancy preserve that

showcases Louisiana's hardwood wetlands, you'll come upon an unexpected find: abandoned ammo dumps left over from World War II. The shape of these old buildings makes you think you've stumbled across an industrial Hobbit site.

Their large green doors all ajar, the bunkers were built in 1939 and were used to store ammunition during World War II and as late as the Korean War. This use was abandoned in 1963.

The Bottomlands Trail, which leads to the ammo dumps, is a 5.5-mile round trip and is a dual trail that meets at small water crossings from time to time. One trail is designated for hikers, the other for horseback riders. The trails are well kept and are clearly marked.

You're out in raw nature here, and although there's a nice parking lot with restrooms at the trail's beginning, keep in mind that the trek to the ammo dumps is 5.5 miles with no facilities or benches: Wear walking shoes and be ready for the physical challenges.

During wartime, the dumps were manned by civilians but the grounds were maintained and secured by Marines on horseback, the reason for today's horseback trail. The horses were eventually replaced by Jeeps.

The ordnance was initially brought in via the Mississippi River and by rail but soon it came in exclusively by rail. The ammo dumps here were used to house the blackpowder used for battleship armaments and torpedo warheads destined for the Pacific during World War II.

The 649-acre property was given jointly to the State of Louisiana, Tulane University and Plaquemines Parish, which now maintains it. It is also the site of the Audubon Center for Research of Endangered Species.

Armadillos on the trail

The Woodland Conservancy's mission is to study and preserve the Louisiana hardwood wetlands. There are signs and trail markers explaining the ecological doings around you. As you follow the trail, you'll come across a variety of plants and animals, none more interesting than the numerous armadillos foraging in the underbrush. They add an unthreatening and pleasant element to the walk and seem totally unfazed by human presence. The Woodland Conservancy is also a spot for educational activities for schoolchildren, with a series of nature walks and events held throughout the year.

ISLEÑOS MUSEUM

*The memory of immigrants who came
from the Canary Islands*

1345 Bayou Road, St. Bernard
504-277-4681
losislenos.org
Wed–Sun 11am–4pm and by appointment

I n a picture-perfect rural setting on Bayou Road in St. Bernard, among wooden houses and stately moss-covered oaks, the Los Isleños Heritage and Multi-Cultural Park is a museum that is really a small complex of historic buildings. Most of the buildings were once inhabited by residents of St. Bernard Parish, who can trace their ancestors directly to the first immigrants to arriving in Louisiana from the Canary Islands in 1778.

The first building of the complex was designed by architects in the spirit of the homes built by the ancestors of the first Isleños. It is equipped with artifacts such as traditional clothes, utensils, tools and other items of everyday use. Many of the items were donated by the Spanish government after the devastation of the complex by Hurricane Katrina.

Next to this building is the DuCros House which serves as a library and meeting room. The house showcases the outdoor culture established here with an emphasis on trapping, hunting and fishing. There are dugout pirogues – the small boats Native Americans showed the first Isleños how to construct to help navigate the swampy bayous.

Other smaller houses that were moved to the park demonstrate the historic architecture of the Isleños.

Two identical houses are built in the typical floor plan and are constructed in a traditional manner. One is up-to-date, the other is left as it may have been when inhabited years ago, with cypress posts and bousillage construction. Bousillage (made from mud, moss and hair) was used as insulation in early southern Louisiana.

Moved here and reassembled just as it was when it was a hub of social and commercial gatherings in the community, the Coconut Barroom is a small rustic bar that can be rented for private events.

A replica of a trapping cabin built by a former trapper, complete with hanging muskrat pelts, gives a real flavor of how it must have been to work this land. There is also a palmetto hut donated by the Houmas Tribe, showing how Native Americans lived in these environs.

Every year the complex is the site of the Los Isleños Festival.

CREVASSE 22

Contemporary art on a tucked-away property

8114 Saro Lane, Poydras
504-218-4807
Free admission
Call ahead for opening times
18.4 miles from New Orleans

At the end of a short suburban road along the Mississippi River levee in St. Bernard Parish, Crevasse 22 (also called the River House) is a whimsical juxtaposition of modern art and nature-inspired creations by well-known south Louisiana artists.

At first you might mistake the tucked-away property for a private home nestled up against the levee. If you come mid-week, you'll probably be the only one there, giving the outdoor space a truly secret feeling. You can tell you've arrived by the multiple sculptures that dot the property.

The 1922 natural crevasse (breach in the levee), which gives the property its name, tragically led to the authorities' mistaken notion that dynamiting the levee during the great flood of 1927 would spare the city of New Orleans from catastrophic flooding. Actually, a crevasse north of New Orleans had alleviated the threat to the city, and this subsequent, truly unnecessary destruction of the levee still reverberates through the history of the area.

Locals Sidney Torres III and Robert Burns, who head the Burns/Torres Trust, chose Creative Alliance of New Orleans' executive director Jeanne Nathan to put together something "interesting" on a site that is only feet away from the Mighty Mississippi. Her idea for the project was to combine nature, art, culture, the human presence, and climate change among other elements. And it works.

The home of changing exhibits, the River House boasts a beautiful wooden spiral staircase reminiscent in style and materials of what you might find in a futuristic traditional trappers' cabin. There are also changing exhibits outside in the extensive sculpture garden, relying heavily on the robust local artists' colony.

Today the sculptures on the lawn are modern all the way, from see-through bubbles surrounding an oak tree to stylized alligators: one doing chin-ups, another fashioned as a bench overlooking peaceful Bayou Terre-aux-Boeufs, where sea birds perched on logs protruding from the bayou or casually soaring above the tranquil waters supply a natural visual touch.

Walking paths take you under Spanish moss-draped oaks and past a real St. Bernard touch: art made from modern skiffs and other marine vehicles.

Also prominently featured on the property is a small grove of citrus trees. This adds to the sense of place as these trees are a signature of the area. If you're there at the right time of year, you could probably just walk up and pick a satsuma or an orange right off the bush in the midst of an outdoor art gallery.

Blending art and nature, the campus is dedicated to education about and awareness of the preservation of the wetlands and the surrounding area's ecology, in a world in the throes of climate upheaval.

HURRICANE KATRINA MEMORIAL ㉔

One of the most atmospheric symbolic artifacts you'll ever see

Shell Beach at Land's End, at the end of Highway 46
50 miles from New Orleans

The Katrina memorial at Shell Beach is one of the most atmospheric symbolic artifacts you'll ever see: It sits at the end of the tangible land and arises from the sea that gives life to the community of St. Bernard.

The memorial – a metallic cross with the stylized face of Jesus – sits a few feet offshore at land's end on Shell Beach. It juts out of the waters joined by a black marble roster of the names of all the citizens of St. Bernard who perished in the flooding of the monster hurricane in 2005.

St. Bernard Parish was one of the Louisiana areas hardest hit by Katrina, but it did not receive as much media attention as New Orleans (which it abuts) even though it was almost entirely under water. Indeed, if the flood lines on New Orleans homes are a literal sign and reminder of Katrina's fury, it's telling that many homes in St. Bernard have no flood lines … because in most cases the houses in this low-lying parish south of New Orleans were completely covered by the floodwaters.

As you drive toward Shell Beach today, you'll see many houses and house trailers now built high in the air in anticipation of future floods. The sight speaks volumes about the vulnerability of coastal communities in an age of heightened climate awareness.

"Sportsman's Paradise"

As you get closer to Shell Beach and the Katrina memorial, you are treated to the picturesque scene of a maritime area dedicated to fishing and shrimping: boat launches, advertisements for oysters by the sack, shrimp for sale, stacks of crab traps, numerous vessels hanging above the water awaiting the next fishing trip, shrimp boats docked after working the Gulf all night. These and other accoutrements of local occupations and pastimes make Louisiana live up to the nickname that for years graced its auto license plates: "Sportsman's Paradise." The shrimp boats, with their unusual design, symbolize a way of life in peril due to climate change.